Off-Grid Living 101

The Ultimate Guide to
Sustainable Homesteading: DIY Projects,
Energy-Independent Systems of Water, Wind
and Solar to Unlock a Life of Freedom and
Self-Reliance

Willow Smart

Cover Design by Henry Adrian

Illustrations by David Phinney

First Edition 2025

Contents

Introduction   V

1. Preparing For Living Off the Grid   1

2. Laying the Foundation for Off-Grid Living   7

3. Land and Environment   15

4. Water Independence   24

5. Solar: Power from the Sun   36

6. Wind and Hydro Energy Solutions   43

7. Sustainable Food Production and Preservation   50

8. DIY Projects for Self-Sufficiency   62

9. Mental Preparedness and Resilience   75

10. Health and Safety   81

11. Emergency Preparedness and Safety   90

12. Navigating Climate and Environmental Challenges   98

13. Financial Sustainability and Resource Management   107

14. Advanced Off-Grid Systems and Innovations   114

Final Thoughts   122

Resources   124

Bibliography   126

Introduction

I came to this way of life via a very circuitous route. It was the mid-1980s. Witnessing rising crime right next door to the house I was renting while in school in central Florida, I wondered if I should be moving back up to New York State. As synchronicity would have it, I happened upon a little-known book *"How to Make $100,000 Farming 25 acres"* by Booker T. Whatley. I decided to pivot and move back up north, where I had attended college prior, and try small-scale farming. My then boyfriend and I drove over 1400 miles to visit Vermont, and I fell in love with it. So much untouched natural beauty, lots of green spaces, and land for farming. I decided right then to move to Vermont instead of New York State. We sold everything about a year later, loaded up a rented U-Haul, and headed north on I-95.

But when I got there, everyone told me it couldn't be done.

University advisors, extension agents, and pretty much everyone I spoke to all said,

"A woman can't do this...."

"It will never work here...."

"There isn't enough sun for solar!...."

"That land is completely unsuited to growing crops...."

Well, that final one? Was true! I bought an abandoned dairy farm and started the process. We learned the lay of the land, literally, and hiked all over the place. The property consists of mixed hardwood forests, ponds, and open fields. Hiking one day, we were captivated by a stunning view of Lake Champlain and the Adirondack Mountains across in New York. Except for one thing: no power way up there! It was then that we decided to research solar living and go off-grid for good. There were no books or mentors back then, not even the internet yet! He chopped trees down daily to make a proper driveway, and ran the chain saw for what seemed like months on end. We rented dozers and excavators. Then, the next task was figuring out how to get large trucks up there to deliver lumber for construction. So little by little, one step at a time, we built a one-bedroom apartment above a three bay garage. We heated with wood that he himself harvested and a small direct vent propane heater. There happens to be a lot of underground water here in fact, so we decided to drill a well. That one was the first, of four more to come.

This was the beginning of a 35-plus-year-long journey. All technologies have changed dramatically since then, including solar panel materials, wind turbines, and the prospects for micro hydropower. There are so many choices and price points now. It is, in my opinion, way easier for entry-level enthusiasts than it once was; anyone can do this. I hope this book will introduce you to some new ideas and ways to accomplish your own dream. It is for beginners, and as such, I am including entry-level DIY projects that anyone can build, even if you have never constructed anything before!

Off-grid living is more than just a lifestyle choice. It also offers independence. It means producing your own power, harvesting rainwater, growing your own food, and living with a reduced environmental footprint. It does require learning new skills and adapting to challenges that may initially seem daunting. For those unfamiliar, it is a way back to the land, where every decision affects the whole.

This handbook offers a thorough approach to sustainable homesteading. It covers topics such as renewable energy, water independence, and food production. But it also addresses often-overlooked challenges, like insect-borne illnesses; health risks rarely found in cities. Mosquitoes and ticks can pose serious health threats when living off-grid and understanding these risks is vital to maintaining a healthy lifestyle.

If you are new to the concept or have already begun steps toward living off grid, this guide will help you meet your needs and empower you along the way.

The layout reflects the multifaceted nature of off-grid living. Beginning with the foundation: land and environment, water, and energy systems. Next, it covers food production, from growing vegetables to raising livestock. Finally, it touches on the mental and emotional preparedness required. Each section contains practical guidance and examples.

Off-grid life is certainly not without its challenges. It requires hard work, adaptability, and a willingness to learn. There will be trials and setbacks as well. But the rewards are just as great. The achievement of creating your own energy, the joy of harvesting food you have grown, and the peace of living in tune with nature are incomparable. Approach this book with an open mind, and be ready to learn its lessons.

As you begin, take heart in knowing that you are not alone. I invite you to step away from the chaos and into a life of freedom and self-reliance. Here's to a new adventure that promises both challenge and fulfillment!

Chapter 1

Preparing For Living Off the Grid

"It is not uncommon for people to spend their whole life waiting to start living."

Eckhart Tolle

Have you ever stood on a mountain top during a hike, surrounded by nothing but wind and rustling leaves? One such moment stands out clearly in my memory. It was early fall when I had left my southern life behind to pursue self-sufficiency. Looking across the valley toward Lake Champlain below, I felt a surge of possibility course through me.

The road to off-grid living begins with transforming your mindset. This chapter explores the mental and emotional groundwork needed for this lifestyle change. You'll discover how to develop self-reliance and embrace challenges as opportunities for growth.

Mindset Shift for Self-Sufficiency

A self-reliant mindset forms the foundation of successful off-grid living. This outlook transforms obstacles into chances for learning and growth.

Consider a winter power outage, for example. Rather than letting frustration take hold, view it as an opportunity to enhance your energy systems. You might explore better battery storage or investigate alternative heating methods. This perspective builds resilience and strengthens your belief in solving problems through learning and experimentation.

The shift from modern conveniences to a simpler life requires significant mental adjustment. Many tasks demand more time and effort than before. Preparing meals from home-grown ingredients or maintaining off-grid systems calls for dedication and patience. You'll develop problem-solving skills specific to off-grid challenges since professional help isn't always readily available. This independence encourages resourcefulness as you learn to create solutions for unique situations.

Embracing mindfulness and minimalism can strengthen your path to self-sufficiency. These practices reduce your dependence on material goods while improving mental clarity. A decluttered space promotes calm and helps you focus on essential needs. Research in the Journal of Positive Psychology suggests that living with less often leads to greater satisfaction. This simpler approach enhances both mental health and daily living quality.

Building connections within the off-grid community proves equally valuable as self-reliance. These relationships offer practical support through skill-sharing and resource exchange. Learning from others' experiences while contributing your own insights creates a rich knowledge base. This network of support helps you navigate complex challenges and provides emotional strength through shared understanding.

Assessing Readiness for Off-Grid Living

The transition to off-grid living requires a thoughtful evaluation of your capabilities, resources, and motivations. Think of this assessment as both a mirror and a compass. It reflects your current abilities while pointing toward future growth. Start by examining essential skills like basic construction, renewable energy knowledge, gardening expertise, and water management. This inventory reveals both your strengths and areas needing development. You might discover that your DIY abilities are strong, yet solar technology remains unfamiliar territory.

Setting realistic goals becomes your next crucial step in this journey. Your steps should include both immediate and long-range targets to maintain steady progress. A short-term goal might focus on mastering solar panel maintenance, while a long-term vision could encompass complete energy independence. These clear objectives create a roadmap for your progress. Remember that small victories build toward larger achievements, strengthening your commitment along the way.

Living off-grid requires significant lifestyle adjustments that bring unexpected rewards. Your daily rhythm will gradually align with nature's cycles. Rising with the sun and winding down at dusk becomes natural, conserving energy while deepening your connection to the environment. Modern technology still plays a role, however. Maintaining access to cell phones and internet proves essential for safety and system monitoring. The key lies in finding balance between self-sufficiency and practical connectivity.

Risk management becomes an essential skill in off-grid living. Preparing for challenges before they arise helps you face them with confidence. My personal experience illustrates this perfectly. During our first year off-grid, a hundred-year ice storm struck our region. Power remained out for weeks, and our solar panels sat unreachable beneath ice on a steep roof. Thanks to our backup generator, we weathered the crisis comfortably. This experience taught us the value of having multiple backup systems.

Your preparation should account for various scenarios. Consider how you'll handle equipment failures, resource shortages, or extreme weather events. Build flexibility into your plans and maintain emergency supplies. This readiness creates a safety net during uncertain times. Think of your preparation as insurance – it might seem excessive until the moment you need it.

Make a Self-Assessment Checklist:

· *Skills Inventory: Construction, Renewable Energy Systems, Gardening, Water Management*

· *Personal Strengths: List areas where you excel.*

· *Areas for Improvement: Identify skills or knowledge gaps.*

· *Short-Term Goals: Learn a new skill or gain new tools.*

· *Long-Term Objectives: Energy independence, food self-sufficiency.*

· *Daily Routine Adjustments: Align with natural cycles and balance technology use.*

· *Risk Management: Contingency planning, flexibility in plans.*

Legal Considerations and Zoning Laws

Understanding the legal aspects of off-grid living removes much of its intimidation factor. Local zoning laws form the foundation of these regulations. These rules guide how you can use your land and what structures you can build. They affect everything from your home's design to the placement of renewable energy systems. Two key terms often appear in these regulations: setbacks, which define required distances between buildings and property lines, and variances, which allow exceptions to standard rules.

A systematic approach works best when researching local regulations. Start with your local government's online resources, where you'll find detailed information about zoning requirements. Local officials can become valuable allies in your projects. They often provide insights about specific requirements for your property that you won't find in general documentation. Consider joining regional off-grid communities and forums as well. These groups offer practical experience with local regulations, which can vary significantly between different areas.

Building permits present common challenges for off-grid structures. Traditional building codes don't always align with unconventional designs like tiny homes or alternative energy systems. You may need to request special exceptions for your off-grid projects. This process typically involves presenting your plans to local boards and explaining how your design meets community standards while offering innovative solutions. Water rights add another layer of complexity in many regions. Securing proper permits for water collection or access to natural sources requires careful planning and documentation.

Renewable energy installations come with their own regulatory requirements. Each solar panel array or wind turbine must comply with local building codes and environmental standards. Understanding these requirements early helps prevent costly delays. Consider consulting with renewable energy professionals who understand local regulations. Their expertise can guide your installation process while ensuring all systems meet legal requirements.

Following legal guidelines creates a strong foundation for sustainable off-grid living. Cutting corners might seem tempting, but violations can lead to fines or forced relocation. Keep a detailed file of all permits, legal documents, and correspondence with authorities. This organization protects you from future disputes and provides clear reference points as you expand your homestead. Stay informed about changing regulations through regular check-ins with local authorities.

Your legal groundwork deserves the same attention as your physical construction. Understanding and following zoning laws creates harmony between your sustainable goals and community standards. This careful approach protects your investment while supporting the broader off-grid movement. As you develop your off-grid systems, let this legal foundation give you confidence to build and grow sustainably.

Chapter 2

Laying the Foundation for Off-Grid Living

"There is more to life than increasing its speed." **Mahatma Gandhi**

Establishing an off-grid lifestyle begins with understanding that, much like an artist putting brush to canvas, you will blend your own creative vision with practical execution. Your approach to off-grid living should reflect your unique circumstances while working toward your aspirations. The key lies in carefully considering what draws you to this lifestyle – perhaps it's the independence that comes from generating your own power, the deep satisfaction of growing food from seed to harvest, or the profound connection with nature that comes from living closer to the land. Whatever your motivations, they will serve as the cornerstone of your journey.

Before taking your first steps toward off-grid living, conducting a thorough lifestyle assessment helps create a realistic foundation for your transition. This assessment involves taking an honest inventory of your current resources and abilities while identifying areas where you'll need to develop new skills. Consider how you currently use energy throughout your day and which modern conveniences you're willing to modify or forego. For instance, if you rely heavily on electric appliances, you'll need to calculate your energy needs carefully and plan accordingly. This might mean investing in a robust solar system or implementing creative solutions like passive solar design for heating and cooling.

The road to off-grid living becomes more manageable when broken down into distinct phases that build upon each other. Think of it as constructing a house – you wouldn't start with the roof before laying the foundation. Your first phase might focus on essential infrastructure, such as installing basic renewable energy systems or establishing reliable water sources. The second phase could involve developing crucial skills, whether that's learning to maintain your power systems or mastering food preservation. The final phase often centers around fine-tuning and optimization, where you might add wind power to complement your solar array or expand your food production capabilities to season extension that covers year-round.

When planning your transition, remember that off-grid living affects everyone in your household differently. A successful transition requires careful consideration of each family member's needs, from dietary requirements to education. Children, for example, can thrive in an off-grid environment when their education is integrated with daily activities. Teaching them about renewable energy while maintaining the solar panels or incorporating mathematics into garden planning creates practical learning experiences that extend beyond traditional classroom walls. Allow time for household adaptation - this period often spans months or even years. In our case, we waited several years after installing solar panels before adding our first wind turbine. This gradual approach builds confidence through each stage.

The psychological aspects of transitioning to off-grid living are just as crucial as the physical preparations. This lifestyle change often requires developing new mental frameworks and coping strategies. The quiet solitude that comes with living off-grid can initially feel isolating but often transforms into opportunities for deep personal growth and reflection. Developing regular practices like journaling about your experiences or setting aside time for meditation can help process the emotional aspects of this significant life change.

Creating Your Off-Grid Vision

This requires careful contemplation of several key aspects. First, examine your primary motivations – are you seeking environmental sustainability, financial independence, or perhaps a simpler way of life? Next, assess your current skill set and identify areas where you need to grow. Consider how you'll adapt your plans to accommodate family members, including children's education and pet care. Finally, think about the psychological tools and support systems you'll need during the transition.

· *What are your primary motivations for pursuing off-grid living?*

· *What skills do you possess, and which do you need to develop?*

· *How will you incorporate the needs of your family, pets, and livestock into your plans?*

· *What strategies will you use to cope with the psychological shifts of this lifestyle?*

The key to success lies in approaching this transition with both patience and flexibility. Unlike many modern conveniences that offer instant gratification, off-grid living teaches us to work with natural rhythms and accept that some processes cannot be rushed. My own experience taught me the value of detailed planning combined with adaptability. Before the internet was invented, I relied on handwritten lists and calendar blocks to organize tasks and track progress, from daily chores to long-term projects like the gardens to include even greenhouse construction!

Financial Planning for Off-Grid Projects

The financial aspect of transitioning to off-grid living requires careful planning and strategic thinking. Think of your financial plan as a roadmap that will guide you through both the initial setup and long-term sustainability of your off-grid lifestyle. This plan begins with a comprehensive budget that accounts for essential systems and infrastructure. When planning your renewable energy system, consider not just the immediate costs of solar panels or wind turbines, but also the long-term expenses of batteries, inverters, and regular maintenance. Water infrastructure, whether it's well drilling or rainwater collection systems, represents another significant investment that requires careful consideration of both immediate and ongoing costs.

Research into funding options can reveal opportunities to make your off-grid dreams more financially accessible. Government incentives for renewable energy installations vary by location but often provide substantial support through tax credits, rebates, or direct grants. These programs can significantly reduce the initial cost of solar or wind power systems. Additionally, the growing popularity of sustainable living has led to the emergence of specialized crowdfunding platforms where you can share your vision and potentially receive community support for specific projects.

Cost-saving strategies become essential tools, helping you maximize the impact of every dollar spent. Consider the value of recycled and salvaged materials – not only do they reduce costs, but they often come with unique character and durability that new materials might lack. For instance, reclaimed lumber can provide both structural integrity and aesthetic appeal while significantly reducing building costs. Many off-grid homesteaders have found success in sourcing materials from demolition sites, salvage yards, and even online marketplaces when others might be upgrading their own systems.

Developing DIY skills serves a dual purpose in your financial strategy. Learning to perform basic maintenance and construction tasks not only reduces immediate costs but also builds long-term resilience. Start with simpler projects like building raised garden beds or installing rain barrels, then gradually work your way up to more complex tasks such as solar panel installation or basic electrical work. Each new skill you master represents future savings in maintenance and repair costs.

The concept of financial sustainability in off-grid living extends beyond mere cost-cutting – it requires developing systems for long-term economic resilience. This means creating multiple streams of potential income or value from your property. Consider how your land and skills might generate resources: excess solar power could be sold back to the grid in some locations, while surplus produce might be sold at local markets or traded with neighbors. Some off-grid homesteaders find success in offering workshops or consulting services, sharing their expertise with others interested in sustainable living.

Build a Supportive Off-Grid Community

While the dream of off-grid living might conjure images of solitary independence, the reality often proves that community connections become more vital than ever. In today's interconnected world, building a supportive network begins long before you make your physical transition. Online communities serve as invaluable resources where experienced off-gridders freely share their successes, failures, and lessons learned. These digital gathering spaces provide opportunities to learn from others' experiences, ask questions, and begin forming relationships with those who share your vision.

The power of knowledge sharing within the off-grid community cannot be overstated. Think of it as creating a living library of practical wisdom, where each member contributes their unique experiences and expertise. These exchanges of information often save newcomers from costly mistakes and accelerate the learning process significantly.

Regular community gatherings serve as support to a thriving off-grid network. Whether organized as formal workshops or casual potluck dinners, these meetings provide opportunities for practical skill sharing and relationship building. Consider hosting or participating in seasonal events that align with natural cycles – spring seed exchanges, summer harvest celebrations, or winter preservation workshops. These gatherings can build practical skills and also create the social bonds necessary for long-term community resilience.

The practice of resource pooling represents one of the most practical aspects of community building. By sharing expensive equipment or coordinating bulk purchases, community members can access resources that might be prohibitively expensive for individuals. For example, a community might share ownership of a portable sawmill, allowing members to process their own lumber at a fraction of the cost of purchasing it individually. Similarly, coordinating bulk orders for solar equipment or building materials can lead to significant savings through volume discounts.

Barter Economy for Skills and Resources

The revival of bartering in off-grid communities represents more than just an alternative to traditional commerce – it embodies a return to relationship-based economics where value is measured in more than monetary terms. This system of exchange allows community members to leverage their unique skills and resources while building stronger social bonds. Understanding how to participate effectively in a barter economy becomes an essential skill for off-grid living.

Successful bartering begins with a clear understanding of what you can offer and what you need. Start by creating an inventory of your skills, products, and available resources. Perhaps you excel at carpentry work, have excess eggs from your chicken coop, or possess specialized tools that others might need occasionally. Next, observe your community to identify potential trading partners whose needs align with your offerings. The key lies in finding mutually beneficial exchanges that create value for both parties.

The art of negotiating fair trades requires both clarity, flexibility and transparency. When proposing a trade, be specific about what you're offering and what you hope to receive in return. For example, instead of making a vague offer to help with garden work, specify that you're willing to spend four hours helping with spring planting in exchange for a share of the harvest or another clearly defined benefit. This specificity helps prevent misunderstandings and ensures both parties feel satisfied with the exchange.

Long-term success in a barter economy depends on building and maintaining trust within your community. Consistently following through on agreements, maintaining high quality in your work or products, and being flexible when circumstances change all contribute to your reputation as a reliable trading partner. Remember that in a barter economy, your reputation becomes a form of currency itself – the more trustworthy you prove to be, the more opportunities for beneficial trades will present themselves.

The practice of bartering extends beyond simple one-to-one exchanges. Many off-grid communities develop sophisticated systems for tracking and facilitating multiple-party trades. For instance, you might provide carpentry work for a neighbor who then offers produce to another community member who, in turn, helps you with equipment maintenance. These complex exchanges strengthen community interdependence and resilience, creating a web of mutual support that enhances everyone's off-grid experience.

Chapter 3

Land and Environment

"L_iberty, when it begins to take root, is a plant of rapid growth." George Washington_

The land you select becomes more than just the physical foundation of your off-grid lifestyle—it becomes where your dreams of self-sufficiency take root and grow. Imagine standing on an undeveloped plot, seeing past its current state to envision the future: gardens full of fresh produce, renewable energy systems harnessing power, and a home that works in harmony with its surroundings. Your choice of land will influence every aspect of your life, from your daily routines to your long-term success.

When evaluating potential properties, access to essential resources takes center stage in decision-making. Water availability stands as perhaps the most crucial consideration—whether it comes from a natural spring, a well, or captured rain, your land must provide reliable access to clean water for both household use and agriculture. While many like the allure of complete isolation, thoughtful consideration should be given to road access and transportation routes. The reality of off-grid living often includes regular trips for supplies, possible medical emergencies, and the initial phase of construction when materials need to be delivered. I can't count the number of times we needed to get to the ER over the years! Finding the sweet spot between seclusion and practical accessibility often becomes one of the most important decisions you'll ever make.

Climate considerations shape every aspect of off-grid living, from energy production to food cultivation. Each region presents its own unique set of challenges and opportunities that will influence your daily life and long-term planning. For example, areas with abundant sunshine might make solar power an obvious choice, but they could also present challenges for water conservation and growing certain crops. Conversely, regions with frequent precipitation might offer excellent opportunities for rainwater harvesting and lush gardens, but might require additional planning for reliable year-round power generation. In Northern Vermont, I was told solar would never work here, as Vermont is one of the states with the fewest sunny days in the nation. Hence our decision to use both solar and wind power, with a backup generator for emergencies or extended cloudy days.

The microclimate of your specific location—the unique weather patterns created by local topography, vegetation, and water bodies—can vary significantly from regional averages. A south-facing slope might create a perfect microclimate for fruit trees, while a north-facing slope on the same property might be better suited to wind breaks. Understanding these nuances helps you make informed decisions about building placement and land use.

Side note: If the climate cannot support growing food year-round, there is always CSA! CSA stands for Community Supported Agriculture, wherein a grower charges a membership fee to provide produce throughout the season, supplementing one's own production. When we started over 30+ years ago, there were no CSAs. Now, they are available in all parts of the USA.

Personal preferences play a vital role in land selection, though they should be balanced against practical considerations. While the remote mountain cabin might call to you, consider how its isolation might affect your ability to maintain community connections or access necessary services. Similarly, while open prairie land might offer unlimited solar potential, think about whether its exposure to elements aligns with your comfort level and building capabilities.

When evaluating potential land, modern tools and traditional wisdom both have their place. Start with detailed topographic maps to understand the lay of the land, water flow patterns, and potential building sites. Soil testing provides crucial information about agricultural potential and construction considerations. Local agricultural extension offices often maintain detailed records about regional growing conditions and pest pressure. Additionally, connecting with neighbors and long-time residents can provide invaluable insights into local challenges and opportunities that might not be immediately apparent.

Evaluating Your Ideal Land

· *What essential resources does your ideal land need to have, and why?*

· *Does the area's climate align with your energy and agricultural plans?*

· *What personal preferences do you have for the landscape and community accessibility?*

· *What tools or resources will you use to assess the viability of your potential land?*

Soil Quality and Its Impact on Sustainable Living

The quality of your soil forms the cornerstone of successful off-grid living, particularly if food production is part of your vision. Think of soil as a living ecosystem rather than just dirt—it's a complex web of minerals, organic matter, microorganisms, and space for air and water. Understanding and nurturing this ecosystem becomes crucial for creating a thriving homestead.

Soil health assessment begins with understanding your land's specific characteristics. Professional soil testing provides detailed information about nutrient levels, pH, and organic matter content. While home testing kits offer quick insights, comprehensive laboratory analysis through your local extension office provides the detailed information needed for long-term planning. This testing reveals not just current conditions but also helps identify any potential challenges or deficiencies that need addressing. Our soil is extremely rocky and shallow to bedrock, so growing certain foods seemed almost impossible. The workaround was to employ various techniques in gardening to make it happen. However, it meant more work to grow a carrot than the grower with river bottom soil down the road.

Building healthy soil takes time, but the investment pays dividends in increased productivity and reduced maintenance needs. Composting stands as one of the most effective ways to enhance soil health, turning kitchen scraps and yard waste into black gold for your garden. Cover cropping, also known as green manuring (planting specific crops to be turned back into the soil) helps prevent erosion while adding organic matter and nutrients.

Permaculture principles extend far beyond basic soil management, offering a comprehensive framework for creating a sustainable and productive homestead. This design philosophy emphasizes observation and thought-ful interaction with natural systems. When faced with challenging soil conditions, for instance, permaculture practitioners might use mulching to build soil fertility gradually, and swales to manage water flow across the landscape. We use lots of swales here as our land is wet, and we must divert water in different directions than it wants to flow by nature; in our case, this prevents erosion and further loss of soil depth.

A key permaculture concept is the creation of beneficial relationships between different elements of your homestead. This interconnected ap-proach reduces waste and labor while increasing overall system efficiency.

Designing Your Homestead Layout

Creating an efficient homestead layout requires careful consideration of both daily practical needs and long-term sustainability goals. The de-sign process begins with extensive observation of your land's natural pat-terns—how water flows across the property, where the sun casts shadows throughout the year, and how wind moves through the landscape. These observations inform crucial decisions about building placement, garden design, and infrastructure development.

Zone planning, a fundamental permaculture concept, organizes your homestead into areas based on how frequently you need to access them. Zone 0 represents your home—the center of daily activity. Zone 1, im-mediately surrounding your home, contains elements requiring daily at-tention like herb gardens, composting systems, and small animal housing. Zone 2 might include fruit trees, berry bushes, and larger garden areas that need regular but less frequent maintenance. Each subsequent zone requires progressively less frequent attention, with Zone 5 often left as wilderness for observation and inspiration.

This thoughtful organization serves multiple purposes. First, it minimizes the energy expended on daily tasks by keeping frequently accessed areas close at hand. Second, it ensures that high-maintenance elements receive adequate attention by making them part of your natural daily patterns. For instance, positioning a kitchen garden near your cooking area makes harvesting fresh herbs and vegetables an efficient part of meal preparation.

Infrastructure placement deserves special attention in your homestead design. Consider how utilities like water and power will be distributed across your property. Gravity-fed water systems, for example, require careful planning to ensure adequate pressure at all points of use. Solar panel placement must balance optimal sun exposure with practical considerations like maintenance access and protection from extreme weather. Orient your home to capture sunlight during the winter months, reducing the need for artificial heating. In the summer, shade trees can cool your home naturally, lowering energy consumption. Planting windbreaks, such as rows of dense shrubs or trees, protect the homestead from harsh winds while enhancing the ecosystem. These elements can shield your structures but also provide habitats for wildlife, enriching the biodiversity of your land. By harmonizing with nature, you create a sustainable and adaptable living environment.

Adapting to Natural Elements: Strategies for Harsh Climates

Success in extreme climates demands understanding weather patterns and developing comprehensive strategies for working with them. Whether facing scorching summers, bitter winters, or dramatic seasonal shifts, your approach must balance immediate comfort with long-term sustainability.

In arid regions, water management becomes paramount to off-grid living. Every aspect of your design should contribute to water conservation and efficient use. Rainwater harvesting extends beyond simple roof collection to include landscape features like swales, berms, and retention basins that slow water's movement across your property, allowing it to seep into the soil slowly. Greywater systems can safely redirect household water from sinks and showers to support landscape irrigation, effectively using each drop of water multiple times before it returns to the natural water cycle.

The challenges of cold climates require a multi-faceted approach to energy efficiency and heat management. Building design plays a crucial role—compact structures with minimal exterior surface area naturally conserve heat better than sprawling layouts. Strategic use of thermal mass, whether through thick masonry walls, stone floors, or water storage, helps regulate indoor temperatures by absorbing heat during the day and releasing it at night. The incorporation of passive solar design principles can dramatically reduce heating needs, while thoughtful window placement and seasonal shading help manage solar gain throughout the year. We designed our house to face south, having the largest windows, and the North side has little to no windows, just enough for ventilation and cross flow in the summer.

Traditional wisdom often offers valuable insights for adapting to harsh climates. Many cold-climate cultures historically used earth-bermed structures or partial underground construction to maintain stable temperatures—principles that can be adapted using modern materials and construction techniques. In cold climates, the challenge shifts to insulation and maintaining warmth. Here, strong North winds and plummeting temperatures demand structures that can retain heat efficiently. Designing with thermal mass structures like earth-sheltered homes can significantly mitigate temperature fluctuations. Similarly, traditional desert architecture provides lessons in natural cooling through strategic ventilation and shade structures that can be incorporated into contemporary designs.

Thoughtful design should also account for seasonal transitions and extreme weather events. Consider how your homestead will handle spring thaws, summer storms, or winter blizzards. Infrastructure like roads and paths should be designed to remain accessible in all weather conditions, while buildings and crucial systems need protection from the most severe conditions your climate might present. Lifestyle adjustments can further enhance comfort and sustainability in extreme climates. Adapting planting schedules and selecting climate-appropriate crops are critical to successful agriculture. In arid zones, choosing drought-resistant plants and implementing permaculture techniques, like mulching, can conserve moisture and improve plant health. In colder climates, opting for cold-hardy varieties and using season-extension tools, such as hoop houses and row covers, can lengthen the growing season. These strategies ensure food production remains viable, even when conditions are less than ideal. Efficient heating and cooling techniques, such as utilizing wood stoves, radiant floor heat, or geothermal systems, provide reliable climate control without excessive energy use in the home.

Carefully select building materials to withstand the rigors of harsh environments. Designing structures to endure high winds or heavy snow involves reinforcing roofs and walls with trusses and shear supports. Materials like reinforced concrete and structural steel can further enhance resilience, ensuring your home withstands the elements. Living far north in a high snow load location, all our outbuildings and barns have steep roofs to ensure snow loads slide off and do not build up too deep, risking a roof collapse.

As we look toward water independence in the next chapter, remember that successful land development is a result of patient observation and thoughtful interaction with natural systems. Take time to understand your property's unique characteristics and patterns before making major changes. The investment in careful planning and design will pay dividends throughout your off-grid lifestyle, creating a homestead that works with nature rather than against it.

Chapter 4

Water Independence

"*L* *ess noise and more green."* ***JRR Tolkien***

Beneath the surface of every piece of land lies an invisible network of water—nature's own plumbing system that has sustained life for millennia. Understanding and accessing this hidden resource transforms theoretical self-sufficiency into practical reality. Water independence stands as perhaps the most crucial cornerstone of off-grid living, freeing you from the constraints and vulnerabilities of municipal systems while connecting you directly to one of Earth's most fundamental cycles.

Well Drilling

The way to water independence often begins underground, where aquifers hold vast reservoirs of clean, renewable water. Well drilling represents both an ancient art and a modern science, requiring careful planning, technical knowledge, and often significant investment. Understanding your options and the factors that influence success helps ensure that your well provides reliable water for years to come.

Three primary types of wells offer different approaches to accessing groundwater, each with its own advantages and ideal conditions. Dug wells, the most traditional approach, involve excavating a wide shaft either by hand or machine until it reaches the water table. These wells excel in areas with high water tables and can be an excellent choice for shallow groundwater accessed through loose soil or soft rock. Their wider diameter allows them to serve as a significant water storage vessel, providing a buffer during periods of heavy use.

Dug Well

Driven wells offer a simpler alternative for accessing shallow water sources, typically in areas with sandy or gravel-rich soil. This method involves driving a small-diameter pipe with a specialized point into the ground until it reaches water-bearing soil layers. While limited in depth—usually to less than 50 feet—driven wells can provide an economical solution in appropriate conditions. Their relatively simple construction makes them particularly suitable for DIY installation in areas with the necessary geology.

Drilled wells represent the most versatile and technologically advanced option, capable of reaching water hundreds or even thousands of feet below the surface. Using either rotary or percussion drilling methods, these wells can penetrate virtually any type of rock or soil to access deep aquifers. While they typically require professional installation and represent a significant investment, drilled wells often provide the most reliable and abundant water supply.

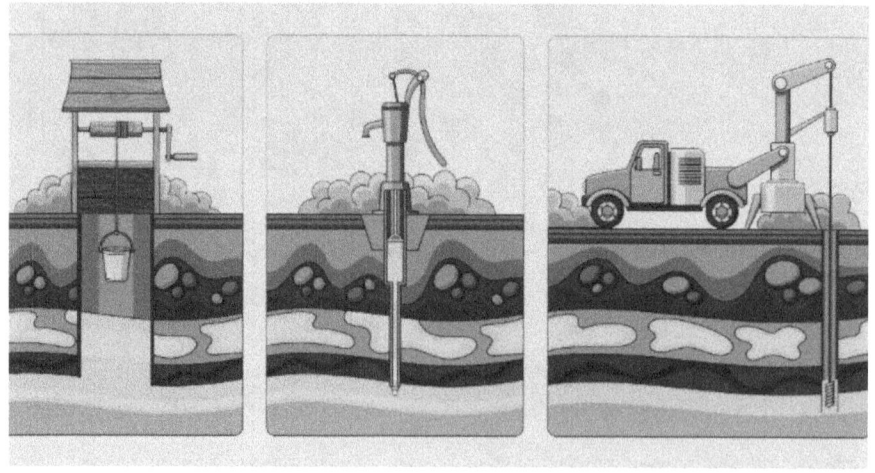

Dug, Driven and Drilled Wells

The success of any well project begins with thorough site evaluation and preparation. Modern geological surveys can provide detailed information about subsurface conditions, helping identify likely aquifer locations and optimal drilling sites. However, traditional methods like dowsing—while controversial in scientific circles—have helped many landowners locate productive well sites. The key lies in gathering as much information as possible about your property's hydrogeology before making significant investments. We used a 'dowser' for all of our 5 wells here on the farm. Form personal experience, they work! For more information, see resources section.

Site preparation extends beyond simply choosing a location. You'll need to consider access routes for drilling equipment, which often includes large trucks and machinery. The proximity to potential contamination sources such as septic systems or agricultural areas must be carefully evaluated. Surface water drainage patterns can affect well water quality and should be factored into site selection. Additionally, consider your future development plans that might impact the well or require additional water supply, as well as any local regulations regarding well placement and construction.

The drilling process itself varies significantly depending on the chosen method and local conditions. Rotary drilling, the most common modern approach, uses a rotating bit combined with drilling fluid to cut through rock and soil while removing debris from the hole. The Baptist Method, a manual drilling technique using PVC pipe and simple tools, offers a DIY alternative for shallow wells in suitable soil conditions. Understanding these methods helps you make informed decisions about which approach best suits your situation.

Water Quality and Well Maintenance

Once your well is operational, maintaining water quality becomes an on-going responsibility. Regular testing should examine both chemical and biological parameters:

- *Bacterial contamination, particularly coliform bacteria*

- *Mineral content and hardness*

- *pH levels*

- *Potential contaminants specific to your area*

- *Turbidity and sediment levels*

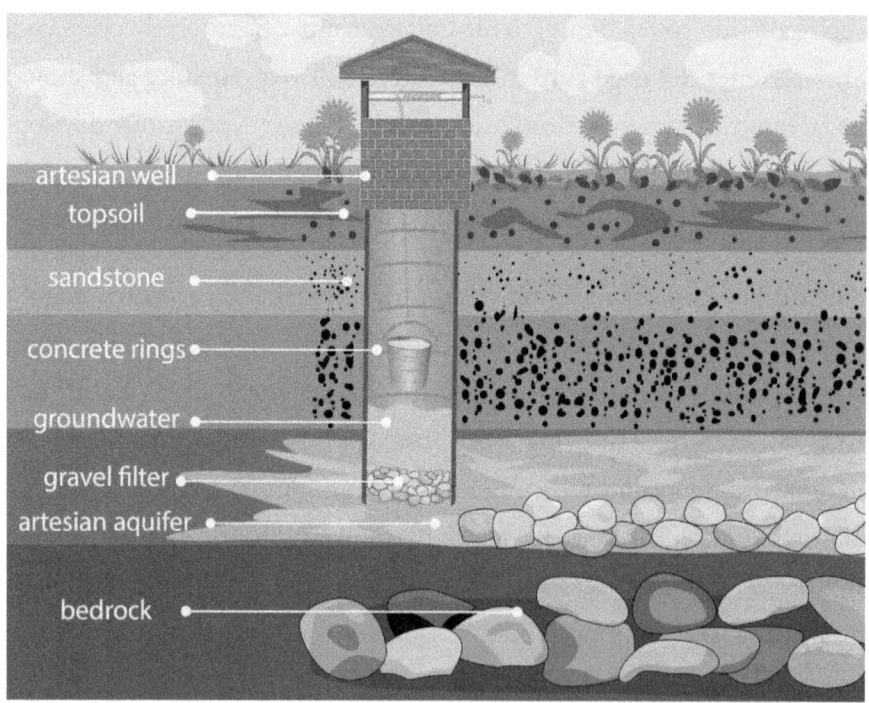

Artesian Well

A comprehensive testing schedule might include monthly bacterial tests and annual chemical analysis, with additional testing after any significant changes in water taste, smell, or appearance. Understanding your water's characteristics helps you implement appropriate treatment systems and maintain safe drinking water.

Rainwater Harvesting: A Sustainable Complement

While wells provide access to groundwater, harvesting rainwater offers another way to capture water before it enters the ground. This ancient practice, refined through modern technology, provides an excellent complement or alternative to well water. A well-designed rainwater harvesting system transforms your property into a water-collecting landscape, making use of nature's delivery system.

The potential for rainwater collection can be substantial. For instance, a 2,000-square-foot roof could collect approximately 1,246 gallons from just one inch of rain. This calculation helps inform decisions about storage capacity and understand your water collection potential throughout the year. The choice of roofing material significantly influences both water quantity and quality. Metal roofs, particularly standing seam designs, provide excellent surfaces for water collection, with their smooth texture maximizing runoff while minimizing the potential for contamination.

The conveyance system that moves water from roof to storage requires thoughtful design and regular maintenance. Gutters and downspouts must be properly sized to handle maximum expected rainfall intensity while maintaining adequate slope to prevent standing water. Installing leaf guards or screens prevents debris accumulation, while first-flush diverters redirect initial runoff containing dust and debris away from storage. Creating smooth transitions between components minimizes water loss and prevents overflow during heavy rains.

Rainwater Harvesting

Storage options range from simple rain barrels to complex underground cistern systems. The choice depends on your water needs, climate, and site conditions. Above-ground tanks offer easier installation and maintenance but may be susceptible to freezing in cold climates. Underground cisterns provide better temperature stability and save space but require more extensive installation work.

Ensuring water quality in rainwater harvesting systems involves multiple steps:

- *Pre-storage filtration to remove debris and contaminants*

- *Storage tank design features like dark, cool conditions to prevent algae growth*

- *Post-storage treatment appropriate for the intended use*

- *Regular system maintenance and cleaning*

Integration with Your Water System

Many successful off-grid properties combine multiple water sources—wells, rainwater collection, and sometimes surface water—to create redundant, resilient water systems. This integrated approach might use rainwater for irrigation and non-potable needs while reserving well water for drinking and cooking. Understanding the strengths and limitations of each source helps you develop an optimal strategy for your own situation.

Regular maintenance is necessary for both well and rainwater systems. Develop a maintenance calendar that includes:

- *Monthly inspection of gutters and downspouts*

- *Quarterly examination of storage tanks and filtration systems*

- *Annual professional well inspection and water quality testing*

- *Seasonal preparation for extreme weather conditions*

Building an Efficient Greywater System

In the pursuit of water independence, one of the most overlooked resources flows right through our homes every day. Greywater—the gently used water from sinks, showers, and washing machines—represents an opportunity to use water twice, extending this precious resource's utility while reducing overall consumption. Unlike blackwater from toilets, greywater contains minimal pathogens and can safely nurture your landscape when properly managed.

Each source of greywater in your home presents unique characteristics that influence how it can be safely reused. Water from bathroom sinks and showers typically contains soap and personal care products, while kitchen sinks carry food particles and cooking residues. Washing machines contribute detergents and clothing fibers, and bathtubs provide relatively clean water that's ideal for garden irrigation. Understanding these variations helps inform the design of an effective recycling system.

Designing an effective greywater system requires careful matching of water sources with appropriate end uses. The system should direct water away from edible portions of plants, using subsurface irrigation or mulch basins to minimize human contact. Consider implementing a branched drain system, which uses gravity to distribute water to multiple locations, or a pumped system for uphill irrigation needs. The key lies in creating a system that requires minimal maintenance while maximizing water reuse potential.

The design must incorporate proper slope in all pipes to prevent standing water, while including accessible cleanouts for maintenance. Appropriate filtering prevents clogging, and automatic diversion systems manage overflow during heavy use or wet weather. Plant selection should focus on species that tolerate the specific characteristics of your greywater, considering factors such as soap content and irregular flow patterns.

Safety and Legal Compliance

Local regulations often govern greywater system design and implementation. Many jurisdictions require permits and specific design features to protect public health. Before beginning installation, research local codes and obtain necessary approvals. This often involves:

- *Submitting detailed plans*

- *Installing required safety features*

- *Following setback requirements from property lines/buildings*

- *Regular system inspections*

- *Maintaining proper documentation*

Water Purification Technologies

Ensuring water safety for consumption requires understanding various purification methods, each offering unique advantages for off-grid applications. The choice of purification method depends on your water source, contamination risks, and available resources.

Boiling remains one of the most reliable purification methods, particularly in emergency situations. This time-tested approach effectively eliminates biological contaminants through thermal disinfection. However, it requires significant energy input and doesn't address chemical contamination or dissolved solids.

Modern filtration technologies offer more comprehensive solutions. Carbon filtration excels at removing chlorine, volatile organic compounds, and many chemicals while improving taste and odor. Though filters require regular replacement, they provide consistent results when properly maintained. Ceramic filters create a physical barrier against bacteria and protozoa, offering a long service life with proper maintenance and the ability to be cleaned and reused multiple times.

UV purification systems provide powerful protection against microorganisms by destroying their DNA, requiring no chemical additives. However, these systems need clear water and a consistent power supply to function effectively. Reverse osmosis offers perhaps the most thorough purification, removing dissolved solids and most contaminants, though it requires significant pressure and produces wastewater as part of the process.

For those seeking economical solutions, DIY filtration systems can provide an effective starting point or backup solution. A carefully constructed sand and gravel filter can significantly improve water quality by removing particulates and some biological contaminants. While not a complete solution for drinking water, these systems serve well as pre-filters or for non-potable applications.

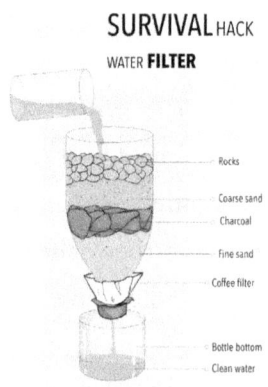

SURVIVAL HACK
WATER **FILTER**

Rocks
Coarse sand
Charcoal
Fine sand
Coffee filter
Bottle bottom
Clean water

Maintaining Legal Compliance

Water rights and collection regulations vary significantly by region, making compliance a crucial aspect of water system design. Surface water rights govern access to streams, ponds, and springs, while groundwater regulations control well drilling and water extraction. Understanding these distinctions helps ensure your systems remain compliant while protecting both your interests and the environment.

Documentation plays a major role in maintaining compliance and system efficacy. Keeping detailed records of system designs, modifications, water quality tests, and maintenance activities provides a valuable resource for troubleshooting and demonstrates responsible stewardship of water resources. Regular monitoring of usage patterns and volumes helps identify potential issues before they become serious problems.

Remember that achieving water independence requires careful attention to both technical and regulatory requirements. Whether managing greywater, purifying drinking water, or navigating water rights, success comes from understanding your options and implementing appropriate solutions for your specific situation. Another crucial component of off-grid living that works hand in hand with water infrastructure to create a sustainable homestead are energy systems.

Chapter 5

Solar: Power from the Sun

*"**S**olar power is the last energy resource that isn't owned yet – nobody taxes the sun yet." Bonnie Raitt*

On a clear day, the Sun delivers an astounding amount of energy to the Earth's surface. This celestial powerhouse, radiating energy from 93 million miles away, offers humanity an inexhaustible source of clean power. By harnessing this energy through solar technology, we can revolutionize our approach to power generation while promoting environmental sustainability.

Battery Storage and Energy Management

Energy storage is the cornerstone of reliable solar power systems. Much like a water reservoir ensures consistent supply during drought, batteries maintain steady power flow when sunlight isn't available. This storage capability transforms intermittent solar energy into a reliable, round-the-clock power source.

Today's solar homes typically choose from three main types of batteries: lead-acid, lithium-ion and lithium iron phosphate (LiFePO4). The traditional option, lead-acid batteries, has served solar homes for decades. When we started our off-grid lifestyle in the 1980s, these were our only choice. They work well and cost less but need regular maintenance and take up considerable space.

Modern alternatives have transformed energy storage. Lithium-ion and lithium iron phosphate (LiFePO4) batteries pack more power into a smaller space and need very little maintenance. While they cost more initially, they typically last longer and work more efficiently. As of 2024, LiFePO4 batteries have become popular because they're safe, long-lasting, and environmentally friendly.

When choosing batteries, consider three key factors: how much power they can store (measured in kilowatt-hours), how long they'll last (measured in charging cycles), and how efficiently they work. Your choice depends on your power needs, budget, and how much maintenance you're willing to do. While better batteries cost more upfront, they often prove more economical over time through reduced maintenance and longer life.

Installing and maintaining battery systems demands attention to safety and technical details. Proper ventilation and temperature control are paramount, as batteries can generate a lot of heat, especially during charging. Ensuring adequate airflow prevents overheating, reducing the risk of damage or failure. Wiring and configuration also play a critical role in optimizing performance. Secure connections and the correct setup of inverters and charge controllers are essential for efficient energy flow and storage.

Regular checks and maintenance keep your system running smoothly, safeguarding your investment and ensuring uninterrupted power.

Energy management systems enhance the efficiency of your solar power system. These systems allow you to monitor energy consumption and adjust usage patterns as needed. Inverters convert the direct current (DC) electricity stored in batteries to alternating current (AC), which is the type that powers most household appliances. Charge controllers regulate the flow of energy into the batteries, preventing overcharging and maximizing their lifespan. Advanced systems offer real-time monitoring, providing insights into energy production and consumption. Modification of usage based on this data then allows you to optimize efficiency, ensuring that your solar power system meets your needs.

Modern solar systems come with Smart controls that manage your power automatically. These systems convert stored energy into the kind your appliances need and prevent damage to your batteries from overcharging. Many even connect to smartphone apps so you can monitor your energy use and production in real time.

Solar Array Design

Before installing solar panels, you need to understand your power needs. Review your electric bills from the past year, noting how your energy use changes with the seasons. Air conditioning in summer or heating in winter can significantly impact your requirements. Local weather patterns matter too – your solar installer can tell you how many hours of good sunlight your location typically receives throughout the year.

Solar panels come in two primary varieties: monocrystalline and poly-crystalline. Monocrystalline panels, with their higher efficiency and sleek appearance, excel in space-constrained installations. Polycrystalline panels offer a more economical solution when space allows for larger arrays. Both technologies can serve your needs effectively and have proven track records. Your choice often depends on your available space and budget.

Thin Film, Monocrystalline and Polycrystalline Panels

Getting the most from your solar investment requires proper panel placement. In North America, panels work best when facing south and tilted at an angle similar to your latitude. Your installer will help determine the optimal position for your location. Nearby trees or buildings can affect performance, so consider both current and future shade patterns when planning your system.

Combining solar energy with existing systems can provide a smooth shift to renewable power. Hybrid systems, which combine solar with wind or micro-hydropower, offer flexibility, ensuring power availability even when solar production is low. At our latitude, 45° North, sun power is low in winter while wind power excels, blowing hard at night. Battery storage solutions complement these systems by storing excess energy generated during peak sunlight hours for use during periods of low to no production. This integration creates a robust energy network that supports your self-sufficiency, reducing reliance on external energy sources and enhancing overall sustainability.

Cost-Effective Panel Installation

While DIY installation can reduce initial costs, professional installation often proves more advantageous. Despite installing our own system in the 1990s due to lack of alternatives, I now strongly recommend professional installation. Certified installers ensure compliance with building codes, optimize system performance, and maintain warranty validity.

Current financial incentives significantly offset installation costs. As of 2024, federal tax credits offer a 30% return on investment for systems installed before 2032. State-level incentives and utility company rebates can further improve the financial equation, making solar adoption increasingly attractive. Professional installation involves several steps. Your installer will evaluate your roof's condition, design the most efficient layout for your panels, handle all necessary permits, and ensure everything meets local building codes. They'll also help you understand your system's operation and maintenance requirements.

Seasonal Maintenance for Efficiency

Like any investment, solar panels need regular care to perform their best. Dust, leaves, and other debris can reduce efficiency, so periodic cleaning helps maintain optimal performance. Use water and a soft brush during cooler morning or evening hours to avoid thermal shock to the panels.

Your solar panels' performance changes with the seasons as the sun's path across the sky shifts. Some mounting systems allow you to adjust the panels' tilt to match these seasonal changes. While not essential, these adjustments can improve your system's output. Many modern systems include monitoring tools that help you track performance and identify when adjustments might help. Altering your panel settings according to the seasons can further optimize their performance. As the sun's angle changes throughout the year, you will need to adjust the tilt of your panels (providing you have this option) to maximize solar exposure. When the sun is higher in the summer, a flatter angle may capture more energy, while a steeper angle is beneficial in the winter when the sun is lower in the sky. By keeping track of these shifts, you can make adjustments to your panel array, improving energy storage. Checking performance fluctuations using solar monitoring software and apps is invaluable. These tools provide real-time data on energy production, allowing you to identify patterns and make informed decisions about adjustments. A review of this data can reveal chances to improve system efficiency, such as recalibrating settings or locating shading issues such as trees growing faster than you had expected.

Protecting your solar system from harsh weather is another vital aspect of maintenance. High winds can threaten their stability, so reinforcing mounts and securing all components is crucial. Consider using additional brackets or support structures in an area prone to strong winds. Snow can also pose a challenge by blocking sunlight coming in and adding weight to the panels. To manage snow loads, install your panels at an angle that encourages snow to slide off naturally. Regularly clearing snow from the panels helps maintain energy production during winter. These preventative measures ensure that your solar system remains hardy and functional, even in the face of adverse weather.

Troubleshooting Common Issues

Most solar problems have straightforward solutions. If your power output drops, first check for obvious issues like shade from growing trees or accumulated debris on the panels. Look for error messages on your inverter (the device that converts solar power into usable household current) and ensure all circuit breakers are in their proper positions.

Some problems require professional help. Professional technicians can diagnose and fix problems quickly, keeping your system running efficiently for decades.

Here's what to watch for:

- *Unexplained drops in power production*

- *Warning lights or error messages on your equipment*

- *Unusual noises from your inverter*

- *Frequent circuit breaker trips*

A properly maintained solar power system can provide reliable energy for 25 years or more. With good care and occasional professional maintenance, your solar investment will continue delivering clean, renewable power while reducing your environmental impact and energy costs.

Remember, switching to solar power isn't just about saving money – it's about taking control of your energy future while contributing to a cleaner planet. Each solar installation brings us closer to sustainability, one homestead at a time.

Chapter 6

Wind and Hydro Energy Solutions

*"**S**he liked the enormous sky and the winds, and the land that you couldn't see to the end of. Everything was so free and big and splendid." **Laura Ingalls Wilder***

Stand in an open field, and you'll feel the invisible power of wind as it gusts. This natural force, when harnessed through modern technology, offers a path to energy independence. Wind is power at work—a renewable resource ready to power your off-grid lifestyle.

Assessing Wind Energy Potential for Your Location

Success with wind energy starts with understanding your site's potential. Not every location has sufficient wind to make a turbine worthwhile, so careful assessment is essential. Begin by examining wind maps from national meteorological agencies, which show regional wind patterns. While these maps provide a general overview, they're just the starting point. For precise measurements, you'll need an anemometer—a device that measures wind speed and direction. Find these tools online or at marine supply stores. By tracking wind patterns at different heights and times, you'll discover your property's true wind potential.

Choosing the right turbine involves matching your needs with site conditions. Wind turbines come in two main types: vertical and horizontal axis. Vertical axis turbines work well in urban settings where space is a challenge, and winds are unpredictable. Horizontal axis turbines, with their traditional propeller-like blades, excel in open areas with steady winds. The power rating, measured in kilowatts (kW), tells you how much electricity the turbine can generate. Select a size that matches your energy needs without exceeding your budget. See Resources section for info.

Horizontal Axis Turbine

Location matters immensely when installing a wind turbine. The ideal spot has few obstacles—no tall trees or buildings to block airflow. Higher ground typically offers stronger, more consistent winds. An elevated position, whether on a hill or platform, can significantly boost energy production. Think of wind like water: it flows best in open channels, unobstructed by barriers.

Before installing any wind system, check local regulations. Different areas have specific rules about turbine height, noise levels, and environmental impact. You'll likely need permits, which may require detailed plans and environmental assessments. Some states enforce stricter regulations than others, so research early to avoid complications. Understanding these requirements protects your investment and ensures compliance with local laws.

Wind Power Output and Calculations

Smaller wind turbines typically produce between 1.5 and 5 kilowatts (kW) at peak performance. However, comparing turbines can be tricky since manufacturers measure peak output at different wind speeds. To understand real-world performance, examine the turbine's power curve—a chart showing electricity production at various wind speeds.

To estimate your turbine's output:

1. Measure your site's average wind speed using an anemometer

2. Check the power curve at that wind speed

3. Calculate monthly or yearly production in kilowatt-hours (kWh)

4. Compare this to your household's energy needs

Micro-Hydro Systems: Power from Water

Water power offers remarkable consistency among renewable energy sources. A micro-hydro system captures water's natural flow, directing it through a pipe called a penstock to spin a turbine. This movement drives a generator, creating electricity day and night, rain or shine. Such systems work best alongside other power sources like solar or wind, creating a reliable energy network.

Success with micro-hydro depends on two key factors: head (vertical drop) and flow (water volume). Head measures the distance water falls, while flow indicates how much water moves through your stream. Together, these determine your potential power output.

A simple formula helps estimate power production:

[net head (feet) × flow (gpm)] ÷ 10 = W (Power or Watts)

Example: your site has a head height of 10 feet and a measured flow of 3 gpm.

10ft x 3gpm=30 ͺ 10=W or in this case 3 Watts

Determining Head: The Vertical Drop

Head height plays a crucial role in micro-hydro power. Sites typically fall into two categories: low head (less than 66 feet) and high head (above 66 feet). Higher drops generate more power with less water, allowing for smaller, more economical equipment. Even modest drops can work—a stream with just 13 inches of water depth might support a small submersible turbine. However, drops below 2 feet rarely prove practical for power generation.

While professional surveys offer the most accurate measurements, you can estimate head height using simple tools. The hose-tube method provides a reliable preliminary assessment:

To measure head using the hose-tube method, you'll need a 50-foot garden hose, funnel, measuring tape, and a helper. Start at your proposed intake point, run the hose downstream, and measure the height difference where water stops flowing. Repeat this process in sections until you reach your planned turbine location. Add these measurements for your total gross head, but subtract an inch or two per section to account for water pressure effects.

For sites with significant elevation changes, an aircraft altimeter offers another measurement option. While less precise than professional surveys, altimeters work well for initial estimates. Remember to account for barometric pressure changes and calibrate your device properly.

Measuring Flow: Water Volume

Flow rate—the amount of water moving through your stream—determines your system's potential output. Local resources often maintain stream flow records. Check with the U.S. Geological Survey, Army Corps of Engineers, Department of Agriculture, or your county engineer for existing data.

When records aren't available, the bucket method offers a straightforward way to measure flow. Simply divert your stream's water into a container and time how quickly it fills. A 5-gallon bucket filling in one minute indicates a 5 gallons-per-minute flow rate. Remember that seasonal changes affect water availability—measure during different times of year for accurate planning.

Designing Your Micro-Hydro System

A well-designed micro-hydro system starts with careful component selection. The intake needs proper screening to keep debris out while capturing maximum water flow. Choose penstock materials that resist pressure and weathering. Match your turbine to your site's characteristics—Pelton wheels excel with high head and low flow, while Kaplan turbines suit low head and high flow conditions. Your generator must align with the turbine's specifications to ensure efficient power conversion.

Most home micro-hydro systems generate up to 100 kilowatts, though a 10-kilowatt setup typically suffices for a small homestead. Regular maintenance keeps these systems running smoothly. Clean intakes, inspect pipes for leaks, and keep moving parts properly lubricated. Create a maintenance schedule and stick to it—prevention costs less than repairs.

Environmental stewardship matters in micro-hydro installation. Design your system to protect aquatic life and maintain water quality. Research local water rights and obtain necessary permits before starting work. Your county engineer can guide you through regulations and connect you with relevant resources.

Integrating Multiple Energy Sources

Combining different renewable energy sources creates a robust power supply. Think of it as nature's backup system—when clouds shade solar panels, wind turbines may be spinning, and your stream continues to flow. This approach, called a hybrid system, provides reliable power through changing conditions.

Smart technology enhances hybrid system performance. Modern inverters automatically select the most efficient power source, while controllers monitor system health. Energy management software provides real-time data about your power production and usage patterns. These tools help you optimize your system's operation and prevent problems before they start.

Battery storage ties your hybrid system together. Proper battery selection balances cost against capacity—you'll need enough storage to power your home through periods of low production. Consider factors like battery type, maintenance requirements, and replacement costs when designing your storage system.

We designed our hilltop homestead with roof-mounted solar panels, a wind turbine, and a backup generator. While our location didn't suit micro-hydro power, combining multiple energy sources ensures reliable power year-round. Each component strengthens the system, creating true energy independence.

Success with renewable energy requires hands-on management. Monitor your system's performance, adjust settings as needed, and stay current with maintenance. This proactive approach maximizes efficiency and extends equipment life. More importantly, it deepens your connection to the natural forces powering your home.

Remember that each site offers unique opportunities for renewable energy. By carefully assessing your resources and choosing appropriate technologies, you can create a sustainable power system that serves your needs while respecting the environment.

Chapter 7

Sustainable Food Production and Preservation

"Cultivate ease and order, not battle disease and disorder..."
Eliot Coleman

Nature offers perfect models for sustainable food production. By observing how natural ecosystems work, we can create productive gardens that largely maintain themselves. This approach, called permaculture, helps us design spaces that work with nature rather than against it. The concept starts with smart planning - organizing your land into zones based on how often you need to access different areas. Kitchen gardens should be close to home, while areas for gathering wild foods can sit farther away. This thoughtful arrangement saves time and energy while making the most of natural resources like sunlight and wind.

Designing a Permaculture Garden

A well-designed permaculture garden mirrors natural woodlands, with plants growing in complementary layers. Tall trees provide shade and shelter, while smaller plants thrive below. Ground covers protect soil and hold moisture. This layered approach creates a 'food forest' - a diverse ecosystem that produces food while supporting itself. Plants work together naturally: some repel pests, others attract beneficial insects, and many share nutrients. Understanding these relationships helps you create a garden that thrives with minimal intervention.

Healthy soil forms the foundation of successful gardening. Mulching - covering soil with organic materials like straw, leaves or even paper - keeps moisture in and weeds out. As mulch breaks down, it enriches the soil naturally. Composting transforms kitchen scraps and yard waste into rich fertilizer, feeding your garden without chemical inputs. These simple practices build soil health over time, leading to more abundant harvests with less work.

Diversity makes gardens resilient. Including many different plant species helps your garden withstand pests and weather challenges. Native plants often work best since they're adapted to local conditions. Flowering plants attract pollinators, boosting garden productivity. Some useful pollinator plants are those in the daisy family, echinacea, butterfly weed, milkweed, and bee balm. By researching plant families that attract the most bee-loving, such as daisies, mints, and legumes, you increase the odds of enhancing the garden's productivity and pest resistance.

Permaculture Checklist

· **Observation and Interaction**: *Observe local ecosystems and note how they function. Consider how you might replicate these processes in your own garden.*

· **Zone and Sector Planning**: *Sketch a garden layout, incorporating zones based on usage and sectors influenced by external energies like sun and wind.*

· **Layering and Companion Planting**: *Choose plants that complement each other and fit into different layers, creating a harmonious and productive environment.*

· **Soil Health Practices**: *Decide on mulching and composting techniques that suit your space and resources, enhancing soil fertility organically.*

· **Biodiversity Goals**: *Plan for various plant species, including perennials and flowering plants, to support a resilient and self-sustaining garden ecosystem.*

Creating a Food Forest

A food forest produces food while largely maintaining itself. Multiple layers of plants support each other, creating a stable ecosystem. Trees provide the upper canopy, while shrubs and smaller plants fill in below. This design maximizes space usage while minimizing maintenance needs.

Start with fruit and nut trees as your forest's foundation. Under these, plant perennial vegetables and fruits like asparagus and berries as long as the trees' canopies do not shade the plants below (do not plant too close to the trees). Add edible shrubs and ground covers to complete the system. Native species are valuable because they are adapted to local conditions and require less care. Their presence enriches the ecosystem, supporting native wildlife and enhancing biodiversity.

Water management is crucial in ensuring the health and productivity of your food forest. Implementing swales and contour planting can help retain water in the landscape, channeling it to where it is most needed. Swales slow and spread water across your garden, reducing runoff and increasing infiltration. Drip irrigation systems utilize efficient watering, delivering moisture directly to plant roots with minimal waste. As a bonus, this targeted approach conserves water and reduces the risk of disease by keeping foliage dry as well. By integrating these systems, you create a hardy garden that can withstand periods of drought while still maintaining productive growth.

Here is a simple raised bed design using three 2x8x8s, 12 16D nails, and some galvanized deck screws.

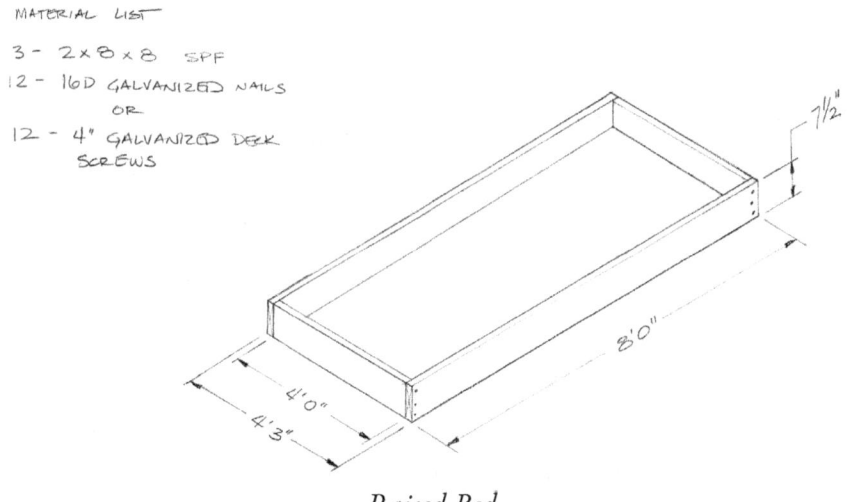

Raised Bed

Maintaining soil fertility with organic matter is the backbone of a thriving food forest. Composting and mulching are essential practices that replenish nutrients and improve soil structure. Composting transforms organic waste into rich humus, which can be spread around plants to enhance growth. The cold frame below allows you to start plants earlier for season extension. Just add an old window or some plastic sheeting for the top. One 4 by 8 sheet of plywood makes two cold frames, measuring 2' by 4'. Cold frames can certainly be built larger, these are designed to be easy to move around for anyone.

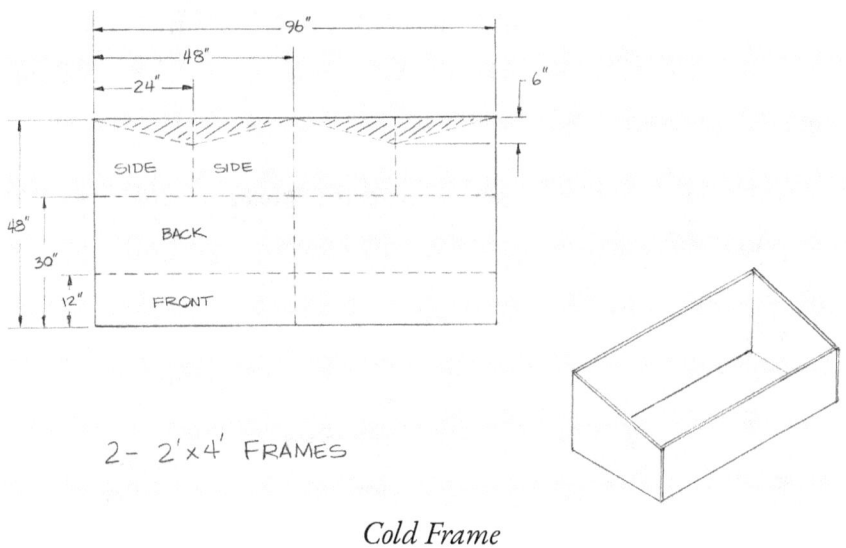

Cold Frame

Soil fertility needs constant attention. Compost adds nutrients, while mulch protects and enriches soil. Plants like clover naturally add nitrogen to soil. Cover crops protect and feed soil between growing seasons. Check your local plant hardiness zone here www.https://planthardiness.ars.usd a.gov/ to choose plants that will thrive in your area.

Canning and Preserving

Preserving the harvest is an addictive practice that connects us to seasonal rhythms. Canning is one of several reliable methods for 'putting up' your garden's bounty. Canning and pickling might be my favorite part of homesteading. I have been canning for over 35 years, and it has been 99.9% foolproof all this time! I had one jar burst just last year. Not bad for so many years.... Canning safely stores food for months or years, using either water bath or pressure methods. Water bath canning is used for acidic foods like jams and pickles, while pressure canning handles low-acid foods like vegetables and meats. Both methods require careful attention to safety and detail.

Homemade Sauerkraut

Fermentation offers another preservation method that also adds gut-healing probiotics. Here's a simple homemade sauerkraut recipe that uses basic fermentation:

Homemade Sauerkraut

Supplies:

Crock or bucket

A plate that fits inside the above

Heavy pot that will fit inside to use as a weight

2.5 lbs. cabbage/ grated or shredded

1.5 tablespoons sea salt

Grate the cabbage by hand or in a food processor. Sprinkle the salt over it in a large bowl and mix thoroughly by hand. Press by hand to release the cabbage's juices, and then put it in the bucket or crock. Press down firmly and then place the plate on top inside the bucket, and using a heavy pot or jug of water, weigh the entire thing down. Store to ferment in a cool, dark place but close by so you can check its development in a few days. After two to three days, check the crock and taste some of the cabbage with a clean wooden spoon. It should be tangy. Repeat this until the desired sourness is to your liking. If a scum develops on the top, simply skim it off with a clean utensil. It is harmless! The entire timeframe is about 2-4 weeks at 70 degrees F. Store in jars in a cool, dark place like a root cellar or refrigerator. I have had sauerkraut that lasted a year in the fridge and was still delicious!

Dehydrating removes moisture from foods while concentrating flavors. Use a dehydrator to desiccate food or air-dry in a warm environment. Herbs can also be dried by hanging upside down in a cool, dark space.

A root cellar uses earth's natural cooling properties for food storage. An ideal cellar maintains temperatures between 32-40°F with high humidity. This environment perfectly suits root vegetables like potatoes and carrots. Your cellar might be as simple as a covered pit or as complex as an underground room with shelves. A cool basement can work well if protected from rodents. Check canned goods regularly for spoilage signs like smells, mold, or off-colors. Label everything with dates and rotate stock using FIFO, the "first in, first out" system.

Natural Pest Control

Garden pests leave clear signs. Aphids cluster on plants, causing them to wilt and die. Beetles destroy plants by chewing holes in leaves, and caterpillars can strip entire plants in a few hours! Quick identification leads to better control. With the magic of the internet, we now even have apps to ID bugs!

Some apps like Seek, Picture Insect, PlantIn, and Insect Identifier make identifying garden visitors easier than ever. These work on both Android and Apple operating systems.

Strategic planting naturally deters pests. Using companion planting, marigolds are believed to protect tomatoes from nematodes, and basil repels aphids from peppers. These companion plants confuse pests with their scents and attract beneficial insects like ladybugs and lacewings that eat harmful insects.

Natural pest control starts in the kitchen.

Homemade Insect Spray (aphids, whiteflies)

Chop four garlic cloves

Add two teaspoons of red pepper (cayenne or chili) or two finely chopped fresh hot peppers

Blend with two cups of water for a minute

Let it steep overnight

Strain the liquid through cheesecloth or a fine kitchen sieve

Add a tablespoon of detergent (I prefer unscented, free of dyes)

Dilute with five cups of water

Add to a sprayer and soak both sides of the leaves

Introducing nematodes—microscopic worms that target larvae—provides an effective solution for soil-dwelling pests. One can purchase these online. However, these can take some time to become effective. Natural remedies also include diatomaceous earth, which desiccates soft-bodied insects, and baking soda solutions to combat fungal issues. Here is a simple recipe to target fungal diseases.

Baking Soda Spray

1 tsp of baking soda

1 liter of water

A couple of drops of liquid soap (this enables the spray to adhere to the leaves)

Add to sprayer and soak both sides of leaves (top and bottom)

These organic options are easy to make and use from simple ingredients already in the pantry!

Create a habitat for natural pest control such as birds, bats, and toads. Garden features like water sources and sheltered areas attract these beneficial predators, building a balanced ecosystem that helps manage pests naturally. By encouraging these predators, you create a self-regulating garden environment where natural enemies control pests. Planting crops that attract pollinators (of which there are many) supports the ecosystem's health. Installing birdhouses and bat boxes encourages birds and bats, which are voracious insect eaters. Toads and frogs, often overlooked, are valuable allies, consuming many slugs, snails, and other insects. Creating habitats with water features or shaded areas invites these predators, enhancing biodiversity and creating a balanced garden ecosystem.

Raising Livestock for Self-Sufficiency

Starting with livestock? Consider chickens or sheep. Chickens provide eggs and meat while helping control garden pests. Not to mention they are humorous and fun to be around! Sheep offer multiple benefits: meat, milk, and wool. Their fiber can become blankets, clothing, or craft materials for sale. I used to have my sheep shorn; then, I would process the wool and send it off to be woven into our farm's own blankets. One can process wool in a myriad of ways. Weaving, knitting, crocheting, and you can even sell it raw!

Proper housing protects your animals and simplifies care. Build sturdy enclosures with secure latches and strong wire mesh to keep predators out. Good ventilation prevents respiratory problems - allow fresh air flow while blocking harsh weather. Regular cleaning maintains animal health and comfort. Chapter 8 provides easy DIY plans for both a lean-to shed and chicken coop designed for beginners.

Designing secure and efficient housing for your livestock is fundamental to their welfare and productivity. Begin by learning predator-proofing techniques. Robust enclosures protect against natural threats such as foxes and raccoons for chickens. Reinforce structures with secure latches and heavy-duty wire mesh to prevent unwanted intrusions. Adequate ventilation is essential to maintain a healthy environment, preventing respiratory issues caused by stagnant air. Ensure that shelters have openings for fresh air while protecting animals from harsh weather. Sanitation is another critical consideration; regular cleaning reduces disease risk and keeps your livestock comfortable and healthy. A well-designed shelter lays the foundation for a thriving and happy herd or flock.

Feeding livestock properly ensures their health and productivity. Rotational grazing lets pastures recover between use and reduces parasite problems. Moving animals between areas ensures fresh forage. Supplement grazing with hay or grain when needed, especially during winter. Each species needs specific nutrients - learn their requirements for optimal health.

Maintaining livestock health requires attention to detail and proactive care. Regular health checks are vital, allowing you to catch potential issues early. Check your local area to learn which vaccinations are needed for your chosen livestock if you decide to add animals to the homestead. Vaccinations protect against common diseases, safeguarding both individual animals and your entire herd. Learn to identify signs of illness, such as changes in appetite or behavior, which often show underlying problems. By the time a sheep has gone completely off-feed, it is often too late. Over time, you will notice subtle changes in their behaviors. By addressing these promptly, you minimize the impact and prevent the spread of disease.

Livestock integrate perfectly with off-grid living. Their manure enriches compost, completing the circle of sustainable food production. However, a homestead can thrive without livestock as well. Local farms often sell manure and compost, and green manures (cover crops) build soil fertility naturally.

Remember that sustainable food production adapts to your needs and resources. Whether you focus on gardens, add some chickens, or develop a food forest, start small and expand as you learn. Each step builds knowledge and confidence while moving you toward greater self-sufficiency.

Note: This overview introduces basic livestock care. For detailed guidance, watch for upcoming books specific to sheep and chicken farming. Meanwhile, reach out with questions about getting started with farm animals.

Chapter 8

DIY Projects for Self-Sufficiency

*"**S**elf-sufficiency is the greatest of all wealth."* **Epicurus**

Below is a list of tools needed for various construction projects to have on hand:

screwdrivers (both flathead and Philips)

level

tape measure

circular saw

claw hammer

nails

screws

framing square

chisels

power drill

utility knife

chalk line

wire cutters

adjustable wrenches

Carpentry is about crafting a space that reflects your vision of self-reliance. Repairing an old barn or building a simple tool shed, understanding carpentry fundamentals empowers you to shape and design your own environment. This skill, deeply rooted in homesteading traditions, connects you to a lineage of craftsmanship that values resourcefulness.

First, one needs to understand wood types and their different uses. Each type of wood offers unique characteristics suitable for different purposes. Softwoods like pine are affordable and easy to work with, making them ideal for temporary structures or interior projects. Hardwoods like oak or maple, known for their durability, are used for furniture or load-bearing structures. Selecting the correct wood is crucial for ensuring the longevity and functionality of your projects. Pair this with essential tools: a saw for cutting, a hammer for joining, and a level for accuracy—and you have the foundation for just about any endeavor.

Basic joinery techniques form the backbone of solid construction. Mastering these techniques—such as mortise and tenon joints for strength or dovetail joints for aesthetics, enables you to build sturdy, enduring structures. With practice, these skills become second nature, turning your vision into reality. A quick internet search and anyone can learn construction joinery needed for a particular project.

Once your projects are in place, ongoing repair and maintenance are necessary to their preservation. Weather, time, and use can each take their toll. Replacing damaged boards or panels restores integrity while sealing and weatherproofing help protect against the elements. Applying a weather-resistant stain or using caulk to seal joints extends the life of your wood, keeping your homestead ready for whatever nature brings. Keep in mind that pressure-treated wood is useful for structures that will be in contact with moisture; it is a personal decision whether to use it in construction projects that house animals or for gardens and greenhouses. On our homestead, we opted to use pressure-treated wood for sills and parts of structures that need to stand up to harsh elements like moisture. However, for raised beds, or cold frames, where plants will be in contact with it, we prefer not to use it. Pressure-treated woods off-gas over time, and one needs to take this into consideration and its effects on our own health.

Build a Root Cellar for Food Storage

Root cellars provide an age-old solution, offering natural refrigeration through the earth's cooling and insulation properties. These maintain stable temperatures and humidity levels, which are essential for preserving produce without electricity. Historically, root cellars have been integral to homesteading, allowing families to store their harvests through harsh winters. Today, modern adaptations make them accessible to anyone looking to reduce reliance on modern conveniences. They create an environment where carrots, potatoes, and beets remain crisp and flavorful for months, retaining the superior quality of homegrown produce.

Designing a root cellar begins with selecting the right location and materials. Choose a site with good drainage to avoid flooding. North-facing slopes are ideal, naturally cooler and often shaded. Materials like stone and wood are traditional choices, providing durability and insulation. Incorporating earth-sheltering techniques, such as burying part of the structure below grade, enhances temperature regulation. Ventilation is crucial to prevent spoilage of your foods. Design a system that allows cool air to enter and warm air to exit, maintaining the ideal conditions for the foods' shelf life. This ensures your root cellar functions effectively, preserving your hard-earned harvest. Air ingress should be low near the floor (where it is cooler) and vented to the outdoors higher as heat rises.

Build shelves to utilize the space applicable to your needs, to accommodate a variety of sizes of produce, such as larger squash, bushels of potatoes, baskets of carrots etc. Certain fruits and vegetables excel in root cellars. Hardy root vegetables like carrots, beets, and potatoes are staples, thriving in the cool, humid environment. Apples, pears, and winter squash also fare well, their flavors intensifying over time. Cabbage and onions, known as long keepers, complement this selection, offering a varied diet through the seasons. This contributes to a well-rounded storage plan, ensuring your root cellar supports your needs year round. If space allows, it can also store canned goods.

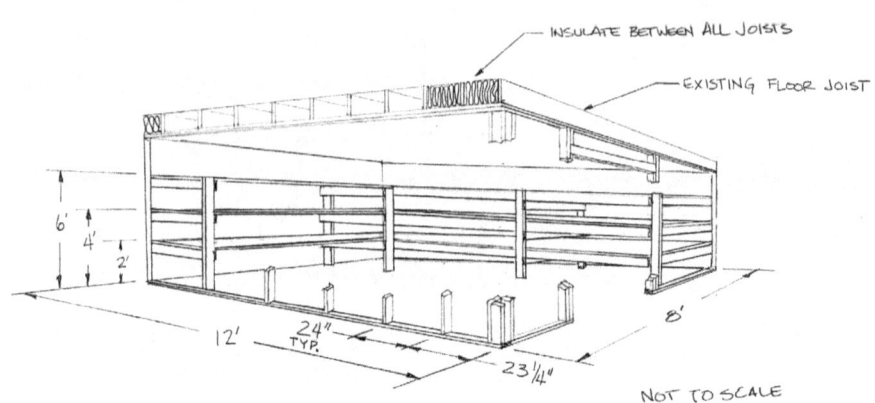

Root Cellar Design in Basement

Build a Greenhouse

A greenhouse can be an integral structure on a homestead, especially in colder climates, extending the growing season and protecting crops from inclement weather. By providing a controlled environment, you can raise crops from seed or transplants all the way through to harvest and possibly save seed for the next crop (given it's a suitable crop to save). An example of this is seeding dill and allowing some of the plants to go to seed. Save some of this seed, and you have next year's dill already on hand! Allowing some squash plants to go to seed would be unsuccessful, however, as they are often hybrids, and the resulting new crop will not be the same type of squash planted the prior season. Greenhouse gardening benefits are profound as it offers a stable climate that encourages growth, and extends the growing season well beyond what nature allows.

Building a simple, cost-effective greenhouse requires thoughtful planning and the right materials. PVC pipes (or metal) form the structure's skeleton, offering strength, while plastic sheeting acts as the skin, capturing sunlight and retaining heat. Wooden frames provide additional support and sturdiness. Begin by assembling your chosen materials for the skeleton by arching the pipes into a series of bows that form the greenhouse's frame. Secure these ribs with the wooden frame, ensuring its stability against wind and weather. Finally, the plastic sheeting is laid over the structure, sealing it to create its own microenvironment. This simplest type of greenhouse is called a 'hoop house.' One only needs to decide the size and how simple to build it or how elaborate to go! More advanced designs have exhaust fans that open on end walls when the interior temperature gets too hot for the plants inside. Ignore this as a beginner and keep it simple. A simple hoop house is just as capable of growing large amounts of food for storage as well as extending the season and protecting plants from predators and certain pests and diseases.

Managing the internal climate is crucial for maintaining an optimal growing environment. Install vents and fans to facilitate air circulation, preventing overheating and ensuring a supply of fresh air. In a simple design, you can use fans as needed instead of permanently installing them in the building. Venting can be as easy as rolling up the plastic sides, or opening doors on either end for air circulation. Employing thermal mass, such as water barrels or stone, can aid in regulating temperature, absorbing heat during the day, and releasing it at night. When selecting crops to grow, consider those that thrive in controlled conditions, such as tomatoes, peppers, and herbs. However, any and all crops can be grown in a greenhouse! Use vertical gardening techniques to maximize space, allowing you to cultivate a diverse array of plants within your greenhouse's footprint. Vertical gardening can be as simple as tent pegs with twine tied at the bottom and then the twine is attached to the upper structure of the greenhouse, or teepees made from sticks or wooden fence posts from a feed store. On heavy crops, like tomatoes, I like to use steel posts from an agricultural store. Vertical gardening allows for more efficient use of space and enables more square feet of food produced per plant.

Hoophouse with Metal Bows Using Vertical Gardening

Build a Chicken Coop

Chickens are invaluable to any homestead, providing a steady supply of eggs and a useful means of pest control. Building a functional and secure chicken coop ensures these benefits. Start with a simple design that includes a coop and a run. The coop should serve as a haven for up to ten chickens, complete with roosting bars for sleeping, perches for resting, and nesting boxes for egg-laying. A movable coop on wheels offers flexibility, allowing you to rotate grazing areas, which helps maintain healthy grass and soil. The 'chicken tractor' model (a mobile chicken coop) is beyond the scope of this book and inherently a more advanced design. However, you can easily find these online if you choose to take the plunge!

Protection from predators is paramount! Design the coop with reinforced wire mesh to guard against foxes, hawks, and raccoons. Ensure that the structure is robust, using solid materials that withstand weather and predators' attempts to breach it. Add a secure latch on the coop door, one that requires more than a curious raccoon to open it. Inside, proper ventilation is mandatory to maintain air quality and prevent respiratory issues, while insulation ensures comfort in colder climates.

The run should provide ample space (8-10 square feet per chicken) for hens to stretch their wings and forage. A covered area within the run offers shelter from rain and sun, contributing to the well-being of your flock. Regular maintenance is essential for a coop's long-term survival. With thoughtful design and care, you are nurturing your hens and homestead in equal measure. I have included a simple design for beginners here. Countless complex designs exist online, so you are limited only by your imagination and budget.

Start by building a heavy-duty rectangular foundation using pressure-treated 6x6s, laid flat and level on the ground. The dimensions should be 12 feet long by 6 feet wide, giving the chickens ample room to roost and nest with a covered run out, while at the same time maintaining their security. Construct the coop's main shelter at one end of the foundation using 2x4 studs framed on 24-inch centers. This supports the entire perimeter structure, from the roof rafters to the metal roof. Use exterior grade plywood, metal roofing, or siding panels to close in the coop's outside walls. This shelter is 6 feet long and 6 feet wide, 8 feet tall in the front, and 7 feet tall in the rear. This serves as sleeping quarters and protects them from predators and the elements. Insulating the walls and ceiling is optional. The choice is yours where to install nesting boxes and roosts. Some efficient chicken coops often have nesting boxes against an outside wall for easy collection by opening a built-in window with a plywood door on a hinge that can be locked safely at night for predator control.

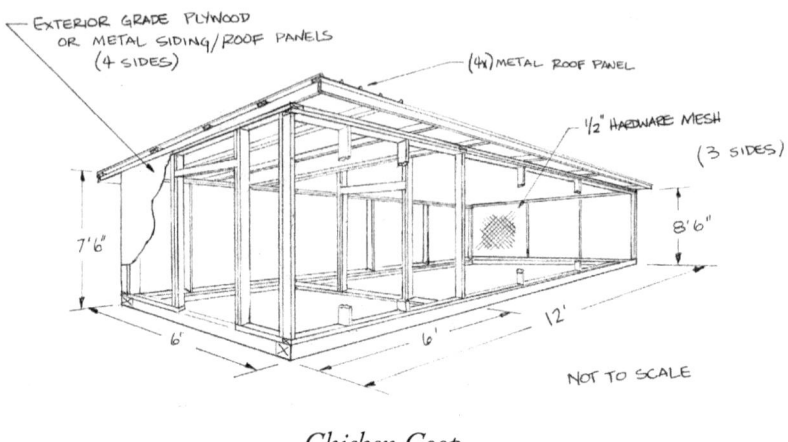

EXTERIOR GRADE PLYWOOD OR METAL SIDING/ROOF PANELS (4 SIDES)

(4x) METAL ROOF PANEL

1/2" HARDWARE MESH (3 SIDES)

7'6"

8'6"

6'

6'

12'

NOT TO SCALE

Chicken Coop

Build a Lean-to-Shed

A lean-to-shed offers a practical solution for those searching for an easy and effective shelter for livestock or temporary storage. Designed with three walls and a sloping roof, this type of shed provides excellent weather protection, protecting animals or crops from the elements. The open side allows for easy access and ventilation, necessary for maintaining a healthy environment for livestock. A dirt floor, even though it is simple, offers natural drainage, preventing water accumulation and helps to keep the inside dry. Whether you are storing hay, tools, vegetables, or providing a resting place for animals, the lean-to-shed is very versatile.

The design of a lean-to-shed is straightforward. Begin by selecting a site with good drainage to prevent water logging and ensure the structure remains stable. Use pressure-treated wood for the sills and untreated wood or plywood for the three walls- this ensures it can withstand the stresses of weather and time. Slope the roof to direct rainwater away from the entrance and cover it with corrugated metal or shingles for durability. In our location, we always choose a metal roofing material for these sheds because of heavy snowfall. With the proper pitch (steep enough), the roof will not allow snow to accumulate and slide off without added labor on our part! This simple design is resilient and capable of enduring most weather challenges.

A lean-to shed is central to homesteading. It requires few materials and little effort, making it ideal for those new to construction or those wanting to incrementally expand their knowledge base. Its utility extends beyond shelter; one can store anything from vegetables to garden tools, a tiller, hay, and even firewood!

Foundation and Layout

The first step is to prepare the area where the shed will stand, ensuring it is level and free of debris. Since this structure will have a dirt floor, there is no need to pour a concrete slab, but it's a good idea to tamp down the soil to create a firm base. Using stakes and string, measure out a 10-by-12-foot rectangle on the ground, delineating the shed's footprint.

Framing the Walls

Start by setting 8 pressure-treated 4x4 posts into the ground, 3 at each of the 10-foot-wide ends. These posts should stand at least 8 feet tall in the back (the lower side) and about 12 feet tall in the front (the higher side), creating a natural slope for rainwater runoff. Secure these posts into the ground with concrete for stability, spacing them 6 feet apart along the length of the shed.

Now, frame the three walls by attaching horizontal 2x6 beams at the top and bottom of the posts and connecting them across the sides and back. To reinforce the frame, add horizontal 2x4s every 24 inches up the walls, giving the structure a solid, weather-resistant backbone.

Installing the Walls

For the walls, use durable, weather-resistant plywood or rough-cut vertical boards and battens for a more rustic feel. Starting from the bottom, nail the plywood panels or planks onto the frame, covering the two 10-foot sides and the 12-foot back wall.

Constructing the Roof

The slope of the roof will follow the angle of the walls, slanting downward from the front to the back (for rain/snow runoff, you don't want it where you enter the front). Using 2x8 rafters, span the length of the shed from the higher front wall to the shorter back wall, spacing them about 48 inches apart.

Once the rafters are in place, fasten with either screws or nails, 2 x 4 x 12 SPF boards, 24 inches apart, onto the top, forming the roof deck. To weatherproof the roof, screw corrugated metal sheets to the 2 x 4s. Another option would be to use shingles, however, metal roof tin lasts longer, and with less maintenance. This shed has a simple overhang on the front to keep out wind and rain.

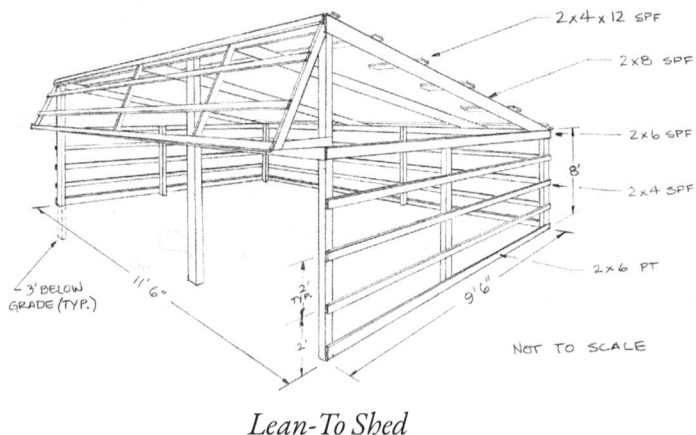

Lean-To Shed

Materials List:

Qty. Item

3- 4x4x16 Pressure-treated boards

5- 4x4x12 pressure-treated boards

6- 2x4x10 SPF boards

15- 2x4x12 SPF boards

2- 2x6x10 SPF boards

1- 2x6x12 SPF board

1- 2x6x12 pressure-treated board

2- 2x6x10 pressure-treated boards

4- 2x8x12 SPF boards

8- metal roof panels 38" wide, length to be determined

Roof screws and nails, as needed

** SPF= spruce, pine, fir board

Chapter 9

Mental Preparedness and Resilience

"No one can make you feel inferior without your consent."
Eleanor Roosevelt

Moving off-grid transforms more than just how you power your home - it reshapes your entire way of life. The switch from conventional living brings both liberation and challenge. While solar panels and rainwater systems mark the physical changes, the mental shift proves equally profound. This new lifestyle demands preparation for both practical tasks and emotional adjustments as you build a self-sufficient life.

Adapting to Lifestyle Changes

The first months off-grid often bring a complex mix of emotions. Initial excitement might give way to stress as you navigate unfamiliar territory. Simple tasks can suddenly seem complex without familiar conveniences. You might feel overwhelmed as you learn new systems, adapt to different routines, and face unexpected challenges. These reactions are completely natural - accepting them as part of the process helps you move forward with greater confidence.

Building a positive mindset becomes essential during this transition. Each small success, from your first successful garden harvest to managing your power system through a cloudy week, builds confidence and capability. These achievements, however modest, mark real progress toward self-reliance. Create regular routines that balance necessary work with adequate rest. Morning meditation or quiet evening walks can anchor your days, while structured task schedules prevent overwhelm and maintain productivity.

Keep a detailed journal to track both challenges and successes. Writing helps process experiences and spot patterns in what works well or needs adjustment. Record how you solve problems - these insights often prove invaluable when facing future challenges. Regular reflection reveals your growth and helps maintain perspective during setbacks. Consider questions like "What challenged me today?" and "How did I overcome obstacles?" This practice builds self-awareness and resilience.

Mental Resilience and Coping Strategies

Off-grid life demands creative problem-solving skills. When standard solutions aren't available, innovation becomes essential. For example, several cloudy days might drain your battery bank - having a backup generator ready shows forethought, but knowing how to conserve power demonstrates adaptability. Study common off-grid challenges before they arise. Research and preparation build confidence in handling unexpected situations.

Remember that perfection isn't the goal - progress is. When projects go sideways or systems fail, focus on learning rather than blame. Each mistake teaches valuable lessons for future success. Share these experiences with other off-gridders through online forums or local meetups. Their collective wisdom offers both practical solutions and emotional support.

Self-compassion plays a vital role in building resilience. Treat yourself with the same understanding you'd offer a friend learning something new. Acknowledge that mastering off-grid living takes time and patience. This mindset creates space for growth and learning without the burden of perfectionism.

Balancing Solitude and Community Connection

Living off-grid offers unique opportunities for solitude and reflection. This quiet time can spark creativity and deepen self-awareness. Take up activities that feed your spirit, like painting, writing, or crafting. These pursuits fill peaceful hours and develop new skills that provide satisfaction.

Yet humans need regular connection. Community involvement prevents isolation and builds support networks. Join local groups, attend workshops, or host occasional gatherings. Today's technology easily bridges physical distance - video calls keep family bonds strong, and online forums can connect you with fellow off-gridders worldwide. Virtual connections complement face-to-face relationships, creating a supportive network that respects your independent lifestyle.

Consider exploring intentional communities - groups of people choosing to live cooperatively, in ecovillages, while they maintain personal independence. These communities demonstrate how sharing resources and knowledge benefits everyone. The Foundation for Intentional Community (www.ic.org) offers extensive information about finding or creating these networks.

Overcoming Isolation Concerns

Watch for signs that solitude has shifted toward isolation. Loss of interest in daily activities or reduced communication with others might signal it's time to increase social connections. Professional support through therapy or counseling can help navigate these feelings - many now offer remote sessions, perfect for off-grid locations.

Try to fill your days with purposeful activities. Local clubs, workshops, or volunteer opportunities provide both social interaction and skill development. Starting personal projects – for example building a greenhouse or learning fiber arts - creates a sense of achievement and satisfaction. These activities offer more than simple distraction - they build competence and confidence while connecting you with others who share your interests.

Technology plays a vital role in maintaining connections. Video calls and messaging apps keep relationships strong across distances. Online forums dedicated to off-grid living provide platforms for sharing experiences, asking questions, and offering support. These digital tools help create a balanced social life that complements your independent lifestyle.

Stress Management Techniques

Off-grid life brings unique stressors. Weather disrupts plans. Equipment needs unexpected repairs. Financial pressures arise. Natural disasters or severe weather can threaten systems you depend on. These challenges require both practical preparation and emotional resilience.

Combat stress with proven relaxation techniques. Deep breathing exercises calm racing thoughts and reduce anxiety. Regular physical activity releases tension and maintains health. Creative pursuits offer emotional outlets and satisfaction. Yoga or tai chi combine movement with mindfulness, promoting both physical and mental well-being. Consider joining local exercise classes for both fitness and social connection.

Remember that mental preparation equals physical readiness in importance. Building emotional resilience through these practices helps you handle challenges while enjoying the rewards of independent living. Your off-grid success depends as much on mental strength as on practical skills - nurture both equally.

Set aside regular time for activities that feed your soul.

River Fishing in Fall

Whether it's reading by the fire, working in your garden, or enjoying a hobby, these moments of peace help maintain perspective and reduce stress. Create spaces in your day for both productivity and relaxation, recognizing that balance sustains long-term success in this lifestyle.

Chapter 10

Health and Safety

"The greatest wealth is health." Virgil

Off-grid living brings us closer to nature's beauty, but it also exposes us to its hazards. Among these, tiny insects pose some of the biggest threats to our wellbeing. These small creatures can dramatically impact health and safety, making protection and prevention essential skills for off-grid life. Understanding these risks helps create effective strategies for staying healthy while living close to nature.

Mosquito and Tick-borne Illnesses

Mosquitoes and ticks carry diseases that can dramatically impact health. Mosquitoes, active both day and night across various climates, transmit several serious illnesses. While malaria primarily affects tropical regions, diseases like dengue, Zika, and West Nile virus appear throughout many parts of the world. West Nile virus symptoms range from mild flu-like discomfort to severe neurological complications. The eastern United States faces equine encephalitis, which can cause brain inflammation. As of 2024, most regions in the country face serious health threats from either mosquitoes or ticks - often both.

Different tick species bring distinct dangers to different regions. Black-legged ticks, lone star ticks, dog ticks, and Rocky Mountain ticks thrive in grassy, brushy, or wooded areas from February through December. Lyme disease, spread by black-legged ticks, starts with flu-like symptoms but can develop into serious long-term health problems if untreated. Rocky Mountain spotted fever brings severe complications without early intervention. The lone star tick, prevalent in southeastern states, can trigger alpha-gal syndrome - an allergy to red meat that permanently alters eating habits.

Black Legged Tick~ Ixodes scapularis

The scope of these threats continues expanding. The CDC estimates 630,000 in the USA contracted Lyme disease from tick bites in 2024 alone. This widespread problem affects both humans and animals, with many household pets testing positive alongside their owners. It is so ubiquitous now, all our dogs are Lyme positive as well as some family members. The rising prevalence of these diseases demands serious attention to prevention and protection.

Strong defenses begin with physical barriers. Install mosquito nets and screens, particularly around sleeping and living areas. High-quality window screens prevent mosquito entry while allowing airflow. For physical protection, EPA-registered repellents containing DEET or Picaridin provide reliable defense. DEET, extensively tested for safety, remains the most effective option at concentrations between 25-30%. Picaridin offers comparable protection with less odor. Those seeking natural alternatives might consider lemon eucalyptus oil, a proven biopesticide offering extended protection. Citronella and other essential oils may help but require more frequent application and careful skin testing.

Strategic landscaping strengthens your protective barrier. Certain plants naturally discourage insects through their scent and properties: lavender, mints, and rosemary can often repel mosquitoes. Plant these around your homestead, but keep in mind their limits in heavily infested areas. Proper water management plays a crucial role - eliminate standing water in containers, gutters, or depressions. Check rain barrels, watering cans, and other water collection systems regularly. Natural water features require careful management through biological controls that target mosquito larvae while preserving beneficial organisms. 'Bt', Bacillus thuringiensis, a bio larvicide, is very effective for mosquito control in water bodies (think barrels, still water ponds etc). Note: in heavily infested areas many of these tactics may be ineffective.

Regular monitoring and quick response saves lives. After spending time outdoors, conduct systematic body checks. Examine all family members and pets, paying special attention to hidden areas where ticks often attach: behind ears, under arms, inside belly buttons, behind knees, and in hair. Keep proper removal tools readily available - the key-style design has proven most effective through 20 years of my own personal use. I keep a "tick tool" everywhere on the farm, in barns, and in the car! Fine-tipped tweezers work well too, but avoid crushing or twisting the tick during removal. Document every tick encounter, noting dates, locations, and any resulting symptoms. This information becomes invaluable if health issues develop later.

Recognizing early warning signs enables rapid response to potential infections. Watch for fever, unusual rashes, muscle pain, or unexplained fatigue. Bulls-eye rashes indicate possible Lyme disease but don't appear in all cases. Joint pain, especially in large joints like knees, may develop weeks after infection. These symptoms warrant immediate medical attention, as early treatment significantly improves outcomes. Maintain a basic medical reference guide that includes common insect-borne illness symptoms and appropriate responses.

Nature's Remedies and Herbal Medicine

Traditional healing practices complement modern medicine when used responsibly. The growing interest in herbal remedies reflects a desire to reduce pharmaceutical dependence while accessing natural healing properties. This balanced approach combines ancient wisdom with new understanding to create a wholistic wellness strategy.

Understanding basic herbal preparation methods opens new possibilities for self-care. Simple water extractions - teas and infusions - represent the easiest technique. Hot infusions work best for leaves and flowers, while cold infusions better preserve delicate plant compounds. Decoctions, which involve simmering tougher plant parts like roots and bark, extract deeper-lying medicinal properties. Tinctures are more concentrated forms, preserving medicinal properties for extended periods, in alcohol. Alcohol-based preparations offer superior shelf stability compared to glycerin versions, which require refrigeration. Proper drying and storage techniques maintain herbal potency throughout the year. Here are some simple ideas to get you started:

· Echinacea, often used to bolster the immune system, can be planted in your garden to prepare teas or tinctures. The process involves harvesting the flowers, leaves, and roots, then drying them for later use. Save them in a sealed container in a cool, dark space.

· Chamomile, known for its calming properties, can be steeped to make a soothing tea that aids sleep and digestion.

· Aloe vera, with its thick, fleshy leaves, is a versatile plant that relieves burns and skin irritations. Cut a leaf and apply the gel to the affected area. Easy to do by leaving an aloe plant next to the kitchen sink for mild burns that happen when cooking!

· Peppermint, another easy to grow plant, relieves headaches and digestive issues. Members of the mint family, such as peppermint, can be used fresh or dried, steeped in hot water to create a refreshing tea.

· Ginger, valued for its anti-inflammatory properties, can be ground into powder or sliced fresh to make a warming tea that aids digestion and reduces nausea. These readily available and easy-to-grow plants offer a natural pharmacy at your fingertips.

Purple Coneflower~ Echinacea purpurea

Poultices are made by crushing fresh herbs and applying them directly to the skin, often wrapped in cloth to maintain contact. This method is effective for treating localized ailments, like bruises or insect bites.

Next time you are out hiking and get a bug bite, pick some plantain leaves, chew it up, and rub it on the bite for a few minutes!

Plantain ~ Plantago major

Safety remains paramount when exploring natural remedies. Herbal remedies, though natural, carry their own risks and contraindications. These can interact with conventional treatments, altering their effectiveness or causing unexpected effects. Some herbs affect blood pressure, or blood clotting - crucial information for anyone on particular medications. Maintain detailed records of any herbal preparations used, including dates, dosages, and observed results. This documentation helps track effectiveness and can help identify potential issues.

Building an herbal medicine cabinet requires careful planning and knowledge. Start with well-documented, widely used herbs known for safety and effectiveness. Research proper identification, harvesting techniques, and preparation methods before expanding your herbal toolkit. Focus on understanding a few herbs thoroughly rather than acquiring superficial knowledge of many. Consider seasonal availability and storage requirements when planning your herbal pharmacy.

Proper storage extends the life and effectiveness of herbal preparations. Designate a cool, dark space for dried herbs and finished preparations. Light, heat, and moisture degrade medicinal properties over time. Store dried herbs in airtight glass containers away from direct sunlight. Label everything clearly with contents, preparation date, and expected shelf life. Tinctures typically last several years when properly stored, while dried herbs maintain potency for about one year. Regularly inspect stored items for any signs of degradation or contamination. Maintain detailed inventory records to track supplies and plan future harvests.

A holistic approach to health extends well beyond herbal remedies. Physical activity, stress management, and proper nutrition form the foundation of lasting wellness. Regular movement maintains strength and flexibility while supporting immune function. Simple exercises like walking, stretching, or gardening provide both physical benefits and stress relief. Stress reduction techniques help maintain emotional balance and mental clarity. Deep breathing exercises, meditation, or quiet time in nature support overall wellbeing. Nutritional awareness ensures your body receives necessary building blocks for health and healing.

Food choices significantly impact overall health. Focus on whole, unprocessed foods rich in natural nutrients. Consider growing nutrient-dense plants that serve both culinary and medicinal purposes. Dark leafy greens provide essential vitamins and minerals. Berries are full of antioxidant properties. Many common kitchen herbs offer therapeutic benefits alongside their culinary properties. This dual-purpose approach maximizes the value of limited growing space while supporting health through daily nutrition.

Developing your health awareness can transform daily habits. Learn to recognize your body's signals and respond appropriately. Notice patterns in energy levels, digestion, and sleep quality. These observations guide preventive measures rather than waiting for problems to develop. Create routines that support overall wellness while preparing for potential health challenges. This proactive stance helps maintain health while living close to nature.

Success in an off-grid life requires balancing traditional wisdom with modern knowledge. Document what works for your situation, adapting general principles to your specific needs. Build connections with healthcare providers who respect both conventional and natural approaches. Create backup plans for various health scenarios, considering both immediate needs and long-term care. Maintain a well-stocked first aid kit that combines standard medical supplies along with herbal and homeopathic preparations.

Natural healing empowers active participation in your health while deepening your environmental connections. This approach to wellness is well-suited to the unique demands of off-grid living, supporting independence while also maintaining safety. Through study and practice, you will develop the skills needed for sustainable health management in your lifestyle. The combination of preventive measures, natural remedies, and modern medical knowledge creates a holistic foundation for maintaining health in most any situation.

Chapter 11

Emergency Preparedness and Safety

*"**D**isaster mitigation... increases the self-reliance of people who are at risk - in other words, it is empowering."* **Ian Davis**

A sudden crack of thunder shatters the tranquility of a typical afternoon. The land floods, the electric grid goes down, and cell towers stop functioning. For those living off-grid, such weather patterns can threaten our very survival. While nature remains unpredictable, proper preparation transforms potential disasters into manageable challenges. As you build self-reliance, understanding emergency preparedness becomes essential.

A Comprehensive Emergency Plan

Assessing potential risks marks the first crucial step toward effective emergency preparedness. Start by identifying natural disasters common to your area - floods, fires, earthquakes, or severe storms. Evaluate your location's specific vulnerabilities, considering factors like elevation for flood risk or nearby forests for fire hazards. Human-related risks require attention as well. Study your property's exposure to potential trespassers or intruders. Consider the physical security of your home and outbuildings. Understanding these specific risks allows you to create targeted preparations for the most pressing threats.

Create detailed response strategies for each identified risk. Map multiple evacuation routes and establish clear meeting points to ensure everyone's safety during natural disasters. Practice these routes monthly with your family. If you have animals, develop specific plans for their evacuation or shelter-in-place needs. Communication becomes vital during emergencies. Establish a network of contacts including neighbors, local authorities, and distant family members. Invest in reliable communication tools - solar-powered radios, hand-crank emergency radios, or HAM radios provide critical information when traditional networks fail. Several modern HAM radio models now offer emergency transmission capabilities without requiring an FCC license.

Your emergency supply kit forms the foundation of preparedness. Stock non-perishable food and water for a minimum of two weeks - aim for three months if possible. Include solar-powered phone chargers and battery banks for essential devices. Store copies of crucial documents - identification, insurance papers, property deeds - in waterproof containers. Review and update your supplies quarterly. Consider special needs: medications, infant supplies, pet food, and specific dietary requirements. Personalize your kit to match your household's unique situation.

Regular practice builds confidence and reveals weaknesses in your emergency plan. Schedule monthly drills to reinforce evacuation procedures and equipment use. These exercises often reveal overlooked details - a blocked exit route or an expired medication. Update your plans to address new circumstances: family additions, mobility changes, or seasonal hazards. Consistent revision and practice transform theoretical plans into practical, reliable responses.

Emergency Plan Checklist

· *Identify Risks: Evaluate natural and man-made threats specific to your location.*

· *Evacuation Routes: Map primary and backup routes; establish meeting points.*

· *Communication Systems: Create contact networks; acquire emergency communication tools.*

· *Supply Kit: Store food, water, fuel, tools, and documents; customize for household needs.*

· *Regular Drills: Practice responses; update procedures based on results.*

Assembling a Bug Out Bag: Essentials for Survival

The concept of a "bug-out bag" transcends survivalist trends, representing a practical necessity for off-grid living. Known also as a "ditch bag," "go bag," or "72-hour kit," this portable emergency pack serves as your lifeline during sudden evacuations. Consider this scenario: a devastating wildfire rushes toward your homestead. You have mere minutes to leave. That carefully packed bag becomes your bridge to safety, sustaining you through the critical first days of displacement while conditions stabilize or help arrives.

When assembling your bug-out bag, prioritize fundamental survival needs. Start with water and food basics. Pack lightweight, high-energy foods like protein bars, dried fruits, and nuts. Consider including MREs (Meals Ready to Eat) for their long shelf life and complete nutrition. Water is crucial - include both stored water and multiple purification methods: filters, tablets, and portable boiling equipment. Your shelter needs come next. Pack a lightweight tarp, emergency blankets, and compact sleeping gear. Include versatile clothing suited to your climate. Sturdy boots, rain gear, and layered clothing options ensure adaptability to changing conditions.

Personalization transforms a basic bug-out bag into a true survival resource. Include necessary medications, eyeglasses, and personal care items. For families with children, pack comfort items like small games or familiar snacks to ease stress. Pet owners need leashes, portable food, and any necessary medications for their animals. Consider including important documents: identification, insurance information, and emergency contacts stored in waterproof containers. Small tools like multi-tools, flashlights, and emergency radios prove invaluable during evacuations.

Regular maintenance keeps your bug-out bag ready for immediate use. Rotate perishable items quarterly, checking expiration dates on food and medications. Adjust clothing and gear seasonally - swap heavy winter clothes for lighter options in spring. Test all equipment: batteries, radios, flashlights, and tools. Replace any damaged or worn items immediately. This systematic care ensures reliability when stakes run the highest. A well-maintained bug-out bag adapts to your changing needs while remaining instantly deployable.

First Aid Skills for Remote Living

Living off-grid means medical help is often further away than a few minutes. Basic first aid knowledge becomes essential, not optional. Start by mastering wound care and bleeding control. Learn proper techniques for cleaning injuries and applying pressure bandages. Understand how to stabilize sprains, breaks, and dislocations using basic materials. Practice assessing injuries: which require immediate professional care versus those you can treat locally. This triage ability proves vital when dealing with multiple injuries or limited resources.

Create a comprehensive first aid kit suited for remote living. Stock beyond basic bandages and antiseptics. Include specialized items: *QuikClot* for severe bleeding, splint materials, and burn treatment supplies. Consider natural alternatives - witch hazel for inflammation, raw Manuka honey for wound care, aloe vera for burns. Homeopathic remedies like arnica ease bruising, and hypericum helps with nerve pain. Add emergency dental supplies and prescription medications. Regularly inspect your kit, replacing expired items and restocking used supplies.

Medical training provides confidence and competence in emergencies. Consider advanced first aid or wilderness medicine courses. Many organizations offer remote-specific medical training. Learn CPR and basic life support - skills that save lives during cardiac emergencies. If you keep firearms, take safety courses covering both operation and injury treatment. These skills build layers of preparedness, enhancing your ability to handle medical situations as appropriately as possible.

Typical off-grid injuries require specific response knowledge. Burns from woodstoves or outdoor cooking demand immediate cooling and proper dressing. Chainsaw injuries need specialized wound care and quick bleeding control. Heat exhaustion often strikes during summer work -

recognize early signs like dizziness and excessive sweating. Hypothermia is a common winter emergency. Understanding gradual rewarming techniques saves lives. Each season carries unique medical challenges requiring specific preparation and knowledge. Research and study these prior to any occurrence in order to be prepared.

Securing Your Off-Grid Home

Remote locations offer privacy but create security challenges. Begin with thorough property assessment. Walk your perimeter, identifying natural access points and vulnerable areas. Consider seasonal changes - dense summer foliage might provide cover for intruders, while winter reveals new sight lines. Install robust physical barriers. Combine fencing with natural deterrents like thorny bushes. Strengthen all entry points with quality locks and reinforced frames. Pay special attention to basement windows and lesser-used doors.

Modern security adapts well to off-grid settings. Solar-powered cameras provide continuous surveillance without grid dependency. Motion-activated lights startle intruders while alerting nearby residents. Consider installing driveway alarms for early warning of approaching vehicles. Simple window and door sensors add interior protection. These systems require minimal power while providing maximum security benefits. Regular maintenance ensures reliable operation when needed most.

Create comprehensive security protocols. Make daily property checks part of your routine. Look for signs of tampering or unusual activity. Build relationships with nearby neighbors, creating informal watch networks. Share emergency contacts and develop alert systems. Train all household members in security procedures - from basic situational awareness to emergency responses. Security becomes a shared responsibility, strengthening overall preparedness.

Wildlife Safety and Deterrence

Living alongside nature brings both beauty and risk. Learn to identify local wildlife threats. Study tracks, scat, and signs of large predators like bears, wolves, or mountain lions. Research seasonal patterns - spring brings hungry bears emerging from hibernation, while winter drives coyotes closer to homes seeking food-or your small animals. Recognize venomous snakes and insects common to your area. Understanding animal behavior patterns helps predict and prevent dangerous encounters.

Prevention starts with habitat management. Store food in secured containers, preferably inside buildings. Clean outdoor cooking areas thoroughly after each use. Manage compost using enclosed bins rather than open piles. Remove fallen fruit promptly from orchards. Consider electric fencing for gardens and livestock areas. Solar-powered fence chargers provide reliable protection without grid power. These preventive measures help reduce wildlife conflicts while preserving coexistence.

Implement effective deterrent systems. Motion-activated sprinklers startle animals without causing harm. Strategic lighting can discourage nighttime visitors. Air horns provide immediate deterrence during close encounters. Install physical barriers around crucial areas such as heavy-duty screens on windows, and reinforced doors on food storage buildings. Create clear sight lines around frequently used paths and working areas. These layers of protection maintain safe boundaries between wildlife and human spaces.

When wildlife encounters occur, stay calm and alert. Maintain eye contact while slowly backing away from predators. Make yourself appear larger by raising arms and speaking firmly. Never run - this triggers chase responses in predatory animals. If attacks occur, fight back aggressively. Carry bear spray when working outdoors in predator country. Report aggressive wildlife to local authorities. While specific defensive tactics vary by species, maintaining awareness and respecting wildlife boundaries prevents most dangerous encounters.

Chapter 12

Navigating Climate and Environmental Challenges

*"**W**eather can kill you so fast. First priority of survival is getting protection from extreme weather."*

Bear Grylls

For those living off-grid, understanding and adapting to nature's rhythms becomes central to survival. While each environment presents unique obstacles, preparation and awareness can transform these challenges into manageable aspects of daily life.

Adapting Off-Grid Living to Varied Climates

Each geographical region demands specific strategies for sustainable living. The desert faces intense heat and minimal rainfall, requiring sophisticated water management systems and careful resource allocation. Shading structures, underground storage, and nighttime ventilation become essential. Mountain residents contend with dramatic temperature swings and heavy snowfall, needing topnotch insulation and careful structural design. Those in humid regions battle moisture constantly - proper ventilation and strategic building orientation prove crucial for preventing mold and maintaining comfort.

Understanding your specific climate zone shapes every aspect of off-grid living. Study local weather patterns, seasonal shifts, and extreme event histories. Monitor temperature fluctuations throughout the year. Note prevailing wind directions and storm patterns. This knowledge helps you design appropriate systems for water collection, energy generation, and food production. Desert homesteaders will need to focus on shade structures and water storage, while those in northern regions must prioritize insulation and snowload management.

Home design must reflect these realities. Passive solar principles work differently across regions. In cold climates, large south-facing windows capture warmth, while deep overhangs shield against summer heat. Earth-bermed or partially buried structures maintain stable temperatures year-round. Strategic placement of thermal mass—concrete/tile floors, stone walls, or water barrels—absorb daytime heat and releases it slowly overnight. These design elements reduce energy needs and also increase comfort.

Material selection directly impacts long-term sustainability. Metal roofing withstands extreme weather while offering excellent rainwater collection surfaces. Proper insulation becomes critical. Water management varies dramatically by region. Arid zones require extensive catchment systems - every drop counts. Large storage tanks, underground cisterns, and efficient filtration systems preserve precious rainfall. However humid areas focus on managing excess - French drains and swales direct water flow while preventing erosion. Northern residents must protect water systems from freezing, using buried lines and insulated storage. Each solution demands careful planning and regular maintenance to ensure reliable water access.

Climate Adaptation

- *Arid Regions: Implement mulching, drought-resistant planting, and rainwater catchment.*

- *Mountain Areas: Emphasize insulation, snow load capacity, and wind protection*

- *Humid Environments: Focus on ventilation, moisture control, and mold prevention.*

- *Coastal Areas: Consider salt resistance, storm protection, and flood mitigation*

- *Northern Regions: Plan for extreme cold, limited sunlight, and snow management*

- *Temperature Fluctuations: Use insulation and thermal mass, and dress in layers.*

- *Climate-Resilient Structures: Incorporate passive solar design and earth-sheltered architecture.*

- **Material Selection:** *Choose weather-resistant roofing and efficient insulation.*

- **Water Management:** *Develop rainwater catchment systems and drainage solutions.*

Managing Energy Needs in Harsh Weather

Extreme weather demands robust energy systems. Start by calculating your worst-case power requirements. Consider essential loads - heating, water pumping, basic lighting, and critical medical equipment. Build redundancy into your system through multiple power sources. Solar panels paired with wind turbines offer complementary generation patterns. Add a backup generator for emergency power during extended severe weather. This multi-tiered approach ensures continuous power despite challenging conditions.

Battery storage becomes crucial during harsh weather periods. Size your battery bank to support essential loads for several days without charging. Modern lithium systems offer excellent performance but require careful temperature management. Lead-acid batteries prove more forgiving but need larger capacity for the same output. Consider creating a separate, climate-controlled space for battery storage to optimize performance and longevity.

Weatherproofing your energy infrastructure prevents weather-related failures. Mount solar panels to withstand high winds and heavy snow loads. Install lightning protection systems to safeguard sensitive electronics. Use marine-grade components in coastal areas to resist salt corrosion. Regular maintenance checks help identify potential weaknesses before severe weather strikes. These precautions protect your investment while ensuring reliable power generation.

Another important aspect of weatherproofing your systems is protecting your components from environmental damage. This prolongs their lifespan and maintains their efficiency. Stabilization techniques are necessary for those using wind energy. Reinforcing the structural integrity of wind turbines ensures they can withstand high winds without compromising their functionality. For extra protection, we added a brake on our turbine in 1995, enabling us to turn it off during winds that might overpower it. It remains functional to this day (2025).

Wind Turbine with Brake

Alternative heating methods provide vital backup during winter storms. Wood stoves offer reliable heat without electricity, while masonry heaters store thermal energy efficiently. Passive solar design reduces heating needs through strategic window placement and thermal mass. Consider backup cooking options - rocket stoves or outdoor kitchens prevent total reliance on electric or gas cooking methods. These alternatives enhance resilience during challenging weather conditions.

Biomass heating is an additional option for those in colder climates. Wood stoves or pellet burners provide consistent heat, using renewable resources available in many regions. Solar thermal systems offer a reliable source of hot water, even during low-sunlight periods. By capturing and storing the sun's thermal energy, these systems ensure you have a steady hot water supply, reducing the strain on your other energy systems. Diversifying your energy sources allows you to adapt to varying conditions, ensuring your home remains powered up.

Harvesting Firewood

As you manage your energy needs in harsh weather, consider the broader implications of your choices. Each decision contributes a piece of the pie, so to speak, to ensure independence and overall efficiency. A balance between preparation and adaptation is essential. By understanding your energy needs, enhancing storage and backup systems, weatherproofing your infrastructure, and exploring alternative options, you position yourself to thrive despite extreme weather, which seems to occur more frequently than ever!

Soil Management for Optimal Food Production

Understanding your soil's unique characteristics is a must for success. Begin with comprehensive soil testing - professional labs provide detailed nutrient analysis beyond basic pH readings. Test multiple locations across your property, as soil composition often varies significantly. Map these results to guide future planting decisions and amendment strategies. Regular testing tracks changes over time, helping you adjust management practices for optimal results.

Building soil fertility requires a multi-faceted approach. Compost forms the foundation - kitchen scraps, yard waste, and agricultural byproducts create rich organic matter. Layer green materials (nitrogen-rich) with brown materials (carbon-rich) to achieve proper decomposition. Consider specialized techniques like vermicomposting or bokashi for faster nutrient cycling. These methods transform waste into valuable soil amendments while reducing environmental impact.

Erosion control protects vital topsoil from wind and water damage. Plant cover crops during fallow periods to maintain soil structure. Install swales on contour to slow water flow across slopes. Use mulch extensively - straw, wood chips, or living ground covers shield soil from harsh elements. These practices preserve soil health while improving water retention and reducing maintenance needs.

Regional climate patterns dictate specific soil management strategies. Arid regions must focus on moisture retention through deep mulching and drought-resistant ground covers and native plants. Wet climates require excellent drainage - raised beds and amended soil prevent waterlogging. Cold regions benefit from season extension techniques like cold frames and high tunnels or hoophouses. Each approach maximizes growing potential within environmental constraints.

Seasonal Adaptations

Success is dependent on alignment with natural cycles. Create detailed seasonal calendars noting frost dates, rainfall patterns, and temperature trends. Plan activities around these patterns - spring planting, summer maintenance, fall harvest, and winter repairs. This organization helps optimize resource use while reducing stress during busy periods. Flexibility is essential, as weather patterns increasingly deviate from historical norms.

Energy management shifts seasonally. Winter demands focus on heating efficiency and snow management of your solar panels. Summer brings cooling challenges and longer daylight for energy generation. Adjust panel angles seasonally to maximize collection. Monitor battery performance as temperature extremes affect storage capacity. These adaptations optimize system performance throughout the year.

Food production requires careful seasonal planning. Start seeds indoors before last frost, extending the growing season. Implement succession planting for continuous harvests. Use season extension devices like cold frames or hoop houses for year-round growing. Preserve your harvest through multiple methods - canning, dehydrating, fermenting, and root cellaring. These strategies ensure food security across the seasons.

Maintenance routines follow seasonal patterns. Spring brings system checks after winter. Summer allows major construction or repair projects. Fall focuses on winterization and harvest activities. Winter provides time for indoor projects and equipment maintenance. Regular inspection and repair prevents small issues from becoming major problems. This proactive approach builds resilience while reducing emergency repairs.

Each season offers unique opportunities and challenges. Success requires understanding your environment's specific demands while remaining adaptable to changing conditions. Through careful observation, thoughtful planning, and consistent maintenance, you can create a sustainable off-grid lifestyle that thrives year-round. Remember that each property presents unique challenges - solutions that work perfectly for one location might need significant modification for another. Experience becomes your best teacher as you adapt these principles to your specific situation.

Chapter 13

Financial Sustainability and Resource Management

"The goal isn't more money. The goal is living life on your terms." Will Rogers

Living independently requires more than just physical resources - it demands careful financial planning and strategic management of your assets. Let's explore how to build a financially sustainable lifestyle that supports your independence.

Understanding the Economics of Renewable Energy

The shift to renewable energy begins with a clear understanding of the costs involved. While the initial investment might seem daunting - around

$30,000 for a standard home solar system - the long-term benefits often justify this upfront expense. Think of it as buying years of electricity in advance. Your system will steadily pay for itself through eliminated utility bills, though you'll need to plan for occasional maintenance costs, like replacing inverters every 10 years even though the solar panels themselves can last 25 years or more.

Making informed decisions about renewable energy requires careful analysis of your specific situation. The time needed to recoup your investment through energy savings typically ranges from 6 to 10 years, depending on your local energy rates and available incentives. Recent developments have made this choice even more attractive - the International Renewable Energy Agency reported that in 2023, the cost of new solar projects dropped by 12% globally. This significant decrease makes solar power an increasingly practical option for many homeowners.

Financial support for renewable energy projects comes in various forms. The U.S. federal solar tax credit allows homeowners to deduct a portion of their installation costs, and many states offer additional incentives. However, it's important to note that these benefits typically apply only to system owners, not those who lease their equipment. Alternative financing options, such as the Property Assessed Clean Energy (PACE) program, can help make renewable energy more accessible by letting you pay through property tax assessments.

Creating a sustainable financial foundation requires detailed planning and foresight. Your budget should account for all anticipated expenses while maintaining a buffer for unexpected costs. This comprehensive approach helps you avoid financial surprises and focus on enjoying the benefits of your self-sufficient lifestyle.

Managing Resources Effectively

The key to independent living lies in understanding which resources deserve your primary attention and investment. Consider your local environment when making these decisions. If you live in an area with abundant sunlight, a solar system becomes essential. Similarly, regions prone to drought require sophisticated water collection and storage solutions. So, two different sides of the coin. In the prior two examples, a homesteader living in an arid region would be benefited by investing in a hybrid system combining solar and water catchment units.

Long Term Financial Planning

Creating a sustainable budget requires looking beyond immediate needs. When planning your solar installation, factor in future expansions as your energy requirements grow. Set aside funds for equipment updates and potential storm damage - nature can be unpredictable, and preparation helps bring peace of mind. Think of this planning as building a financial safety net that lets you focus on developing your independent lifestyle rather than worrying about unexpected expenses.

Making the Most of Resources

Resourcefulness becomes second nature when living independently. Local community swap meets and freecycle groups often reveal hidden goodies - from building materials to appliances that need minor repairs. Your land itself might offer valuable resources. Consider how early settlers viewed their property: trees become lumber, clay is made into bricks, and stones cleared from fields find new life in construction projects. On our own farm, we harvested stones from our extremely rocky soil to build a two-sided chimney, serving woodstoves on opposite sides of an open floor plan house.

Creativity extends to everyday items as well. Those empty glass jars cluttering your cabinets can become an organized storage system. That old wooden ladder you've been meaning to dispose of? It might make a perfect rustic bookshelf. Buying non-perishable items in bulk serves two purposes: it reduces your costs and creates a reliable stockpile for challenging times, such as during extreme weather events.

Income Generation Off-Grid

The 21st century has opened up new possibilities for earning while maintaining an independent lifestyle. The COVID-19 pandemic revealed that remote work extends far beyond traditional office jobs - now encompassing fields we never imagined could be done from home. Your skills might translate well to freelance opportunities in writing, web design, or virtual assistance. If you enjoy sharing knowledge, consider online tutoring, where you can connect with students worldwide while working from your homestead.

Your independent lifestyle itself can become a source of income. The growing interest in natural, handmade products creates opportunities to sell your homestead's bounty. Local farmers' markets appreciate home-made preserves and fresh-baked goods. Handcrafted items - from knitwear to pottery - find buyers through online marketplaces like Etsy, where customers value unique, artisanal creations.

Community-Supported Agriculture (CSA) is another avenue for generating income. By providing seasonal produce subscriptions to local families, you create a reliable revenue stream while supporting your community's access to fresh, organic food. If managing an entire CSA feels overwhelming, consider renting part of your land to experienced farmers. This arrangement generates income while allowing you to maintain focus on other aspects of your homestead.

Social media platforms have become powerful tools for connecting with customers who share your values. Building an online presence allows you to share your story, showcase your products, and engage with a community interested in sustainable living. These relationships often extend beyond sales, creating valuable networks of like-minded individuals.

Smart Resource Management

Effective resource management starts with organization. A well-designed inventory system helps track food supplies and prevent waste. Simple but crucial practices, like labeling items with expiration dates, can greatly reduce spoilage. Understanding your energy usage patterns through smart meters helps identify opportunities for conservation. This knowledge empowers you to make informed decisions about resource allocation.

Today's technology offers accessible tools for managing resources efficiently. Basic spreadsheet software becomes a powerful ally in tracking expenses and planning budgets. Scheduling tools like those found on smartphones help coordinate projects and maintain momentum. These tech savvy aids free up time for other activities while ensuring nothing falls through the cracks.

Sustainable living inherently encourages waste reduction. Creating a dedicated recycling station is necessary for responsible material disposal. A composting system transforms kitchen scraps into garden gold, completing the cycle of food production. View discarded items with new eyes – a discarded window might extend your growing season as a cold frame cover, while used and empty barrels collect precious rainwater.

Finding Balance

Successfully combining work with homestead responsibilities requires thoughtful organization. There are too many tasks and chores, it can become stressful quickly! Designate specific work hours to maintain focus and productivity. Creating distinct workspaces - even if it's just a dedicated corner - helps achieve this during work tasks. Inevitably, a physical space reserved for work helps your mind shift gears, enabling you to concentrate without distracting daily chores or the allure of the outdoors. I can't tell you how many times the woods lured me to go on a walk when I should have been working on something else, like writing my weekly article for the local paper!

Effective time management is crucial for juggling multiple roles. Prioritizing tasks with to-do lists can streamline your day, helping you focus on what truly matters. Lists help organize your thoughts, breaking down large projects into manageable steps. Perhaps implement the *Pomodoro Technique*, which uses short, focused work sessions followed by brief breaks and has been shown to boost productivity.

The *Pomodoro Technique*, named after a tomato-shaped kitchen timer by the Italian student who invented it, offers an easy approach to time management. It alternates 25-minute focused work periods with short breaks. This helps to maintain productivity without burnout. After completing four work sessions, take a longer 15-minute break to recharge. How-to:

Pomodoro Technique

Focus on a task for 25 minutes, set a timer

Take a 5-minute break

After every four of these 25-minute intervals, take a 15-minute break

Flexibility remains essential in this lifestyle. Some days may call for more time in the garden, while others demand inside work time. Allowing this variability in your schedule while maintaining basic chores creates a sustainable balance that supports your independence and financial stability.

Remember that financial sustainability and resource management work together as fundamental elements of independent living. The strategies described here lay the groundwork for a self-reliant life.

Chapter 14

Advanced Off-Grid Systems and Innovations

"Chop your own wood and it will warm you twice." Henry Ford

The year 2025 stands at an exciting crossroads where digital innovation meets sustainable living. Modern technology has transformed traditional off-grid lifestyles into sophisticated, efficient systems that enhance independence while honoring our connection to the land. This is more than just adding gadgets to an off-grid home. This is creating intelligent, responsive environments that work with nature while maximizing resource efficiency.

Smart Systems Integration

Imagine waking up in a home that anticipates your needs. Today's smart technology makes this possible through sophisticated monitoring and automation systems that can be controlled from anywhere in the world. Modern smart homes combine multiple technologies and feature:

- *Energy Management Systems that monitor and optimize power consumption in real-time*

- *Automated Climate Control that adjusts to weather patterns and personal preferences*

- *Intelligent Lighting that responds to natural light levels and daily routines*

- *Water Monitoring that provides detailed consumption analytics and leak detection*

- *Remote Access that allows system management from any location with internet connectivity*

These systems don't just offer convenience - they fundamentally transform how we interact with our off-grid environments. Smart thermostats, for example, learn your temperature preferences throughout the day and adjust automatically, while sophisticated lighting systems coordinate with natural light patterns to minimize energy use. Water monitoring systems track usage, helping you identify and eliminate waste while ensuring your water resources last through dry periods.

The choice of suitable smart devices for an off-grid environment requires careful consideration of several key factors. First, evaluate your power consumption - each device should offer significant benefits that justify its energy use. Look for thermostats that operate independently of traditional power grids while offering robust remote control capabilities through mobile apps. Many manufacturers now design their products with off-grid compatibility in mind, featuring low-power modes and backup battery systems that ensure continuous operation even during primary power fluctuations.

Smart grids and *microgrids* represent perhaps the most significant advancement in off-grid power management. These sophisticated systems use artificial intelligence to distribute energy precisely where and when it's needed most. Through load balancing and demand response technology, they can achieve the following:

• *Automatically shift power to critical systems during peak usage*

• *Store excess energy during high production periods*

• *Regulate power flow to prevent system overload*

• *Enable energy sharing between connected buildings or systems*

• *Provide detailed analytics for system optimization*

If you decide to live with a grid-tied setup that maintains a connection to local power, this allows you to sell excess energy back to the grid. Or you can opt for complete independence with a standalone system. Each choice offers unique advantages - grid-tied systems provide backup security and potential income, while standalone systems offer total energy independence.

The standalone nature of off-grid systems makes cybersecurity essential. Think of your system as a fortress that requires multiple layers of protection. Just as you secure your physical property, your digital infrastructure needs equally strong protection. A comprehensive security approach must include:

• *Robust firewalls that monitor and control all network traffic*

• *Encrypted communications for all remote access*

• *Regular software and firmware updates to patch vulnerabilities*

• *Continuous system monitoring for unusual activity*

• *Secure backup systems for critical data*

• *Multi-factor authentication for all access points*

Modern Ai (artificial intelligence) and machine learning technologies add another layer of protection by learning normal system patterns and flagging unusual activities before they become problems. These systems can detect potential intrusions, predict equipment failures, and automatically adjust security protocols based on perceived threats.

Innovations in Energy Storage

The evolution of energy storage technologies has opened remarkable new possibilities for reliable off-grid power. While lithium-ion batteries continue to serve as the foundation of many systems, their limitations have sparked innovation in several exciting directions. Traditional lithium-ion batteries show proven reliability with compact storage, long lifespan (typically 10-15 years), quick charging capabilities and decreasing costs as technology matures. However, emerging technologies are expanding our options significantly. Solid-state batteries represent a major leap forward, replacing liquid electrolytes with solid materials. This seemingly simple change yields impressive benefits-improved safety due to eliminated leak risks, higher energy density allowing more power in less space, and extended operational life. For off-grid homesteads, this means more reliable power storage with reduced maintenance concerns.

Flow batteries are an especially intriguing solution for those needing substantial storage. Unlike conventional batteries, they store energy in liquid electrolytes housed in external tanks. Imagine two large containers of specialized liquids that store energy through chemical reactions. This unique design offers remarkable flexibility. To expand your storage capacity, it's as simple as increasing tank size. Some advantages include unlimited cycling, lower fire risk compared to lithium-ion, longer lifetime (20+ years) and the ability to store energy for extended periods.

Advanced battery management systems serve as the overseers of these storage solutions, continuously monitoring multiple factors. These management systems can monitor cell voltage, temperature, discharge/charge rates and overall efficiency. They can even monitor individual cell health and usage patterns and trends. As they adjust charging cycles in real-time, they serve to prevent damage like overcharging.

Alternative storage technologies continue to emerge. Hydrogen fuel cells convert chemical energy into electricity through a process that produces only water as a byproduct. Hydrogen technology's advantages are continuous power generation, zero harmful emissions, and quick refueling. Interestingly, they also are scalable from small to large applications.

Compressed air energy storage (CAES) systems offer an innovative approach by storing energy in the form of pressurized air in underground caverns or specialized tanks. When power is needed, this air is released through turbines to generate electricity - a simple yet effective solution for large-scale storage.

Hybrid systems that combine multiple energy sources and storage technologies offer perhaps the most promising path forward. By integrating solar panels, wind turbines, and various storage solutions, these systems provide reliable power regardless of weather conditions or time of day. They can automatically switch between sources and storage methods to maintain optimal efficiency while ensuring uninterrupted power supply.

Future Trends in Off-Grid Living

Artificial intelligence is revolutionizing how we maintain and operate off-grid systems. An AI system functions like a caretaker, continuously monitoring your entire setup through an array of sophisticated sensors. This assistant can predict when your solar panels need cleaning by analyzing subtle changes in the power output, or alert you to potential battery issues before they become problems. The system learns from your usage patterns, making increasingly accurate predictions about maintenance needs and energy consumption. Their capabilities are predictive maintenance scheduling based on real-time data, system optimization for maximum efficiency, and early warning for potential equipment failures. Using weather pattern analysis for optimal energy collection, they can improve resource allocation and integrate seamlessly with smart home systems.

Blockchain technology is creating entirely new possibilities for energy independence through secure, decentralized networks. This system works much like a ledger, recording every energy transaction with accuracy. You would be able to sell your excess solar power directly to neighbors through an automated system that handles all the billing and distribution! This peer-to-peer trading eliminates middlemen and encourages community energy independence. This involves secure energy trading, auto pay systems, and transparent tracking of energy production/consumption. Blockchain would also have decentralized control of community microgrids and verifiable renewable energy credits.

Construction methods and materials continue to evolve, incorporating both time-tested techniques and cutting-edge ideas. Modern off-grid homes increasingly use recycled and upcycled materials in creative ways. Innovations such as walls insulated with recycled denim offer superior sound dampening and thermal properties while keeping textiles out of landfills. Reclaimed wood finds new life as structural elements and finishing touches, each piece telling its own story while reducing its environmental impact.

Prefabricated modular homes represent another exciting development in off-grid construction. These homes arrive in sections, dramatically reducing construction labor and site impact. Despite their quick assembly, they offer numerous customization options. Each module can be designed to maximize natural light, optimize airflow, and incorporate sustainable materials. This combines the best of modern manufacturing with environmental consciousness.

Community-based initiatives are reshaping how we think about off-grid living. Co-housing developments and ecovillages demonstrate the power of shared resources and collective wisdom. These communities often feature shared renewable energy systems, community gardens, and collective water harvesting infrastructure. There are common spaces for social interaction, shared tools/equipment and knowledge exchange programs.

The benefits extend well beyond resource efficiency. These communities build strong social bonds and resilience through mutual support. Members can share skills and experiences, creating a rich learning environment for everyone involved.

In addition, government policies and regulations increasingly recognize and support off-grid living solutions. Financial incentives make sustainable technologies more accessible by offering tax credits for installations, grants, and rebates for water conservation systems. Possibilities also include low-interest loans for conversions to off-grid, and incentives for energy efficient appliances.

Zoning laws continue to evolve to accommodate alternative housing solutions. Building codes increasingly recognize and support sustainable construction methods. These regulatory changes reflect growing awareness of environmental challenges and the vital role off-grid living plays in addressing them.

The future of off-grid living emerges as a blend of advanced technology and environmental stewardship. Each innovation builds on existing principles while opening new possibilities for sustainable, independent living. As these technologies develop and become more accessible, they create opportunities for anyone seeking a self-reliant lifestyle.

Successful off-grid living isn't about adopting every new technology that comes along. One must choose and integrate solutions that align with one's own goals and values. If you're drawn to cutting-edge AI systems or prefer simpler solutions, the expanding range of options means you can create a system that perfectly suits your needs while contributing to a more sustainable future.

Final Thoughts

My vision for this book is to empower you as a beginner with the knowledge and tools necessary to embrace off-grid living. By providing some practical guidance, I hope to equip you with the means to pursue self-sufficiency and sustainability. My aim is to inspire you toward a lifestyle that offers freedom and independence from conventional systems.

We have examined various aspects of off-grid living. Energy independence illustrated how solar, wind, and hydropower can help you break free from the traditional grid. We focused on resiliency strategies to overcome unpredictable natural events and unexpected difficulties. Self-reliance is a key element, stressing the importance of cultivating skills that enable you to live independently.

I hope this book's key takeaways are its practical steps and philosophical insights. Living at your own pace is achievable, and it's vital to approach this transition gradually. Otherwise, complete overwhelm can set in! By setting realistic goals and building upon them, you can slowly increase your independence from the grid, I assure you. Remember that off-grid living is not a one-size-fits-all template. Tailor it to fit your own needs and circumstances, allowing you to transition into the lifestyle comfortably and at your own pace.

Now, I encourage you to take what you have learned and put it into practice. Start setting up your new lifestyle just one step at a time. Whether installing a rainwater harvesting system, planting a garden, or building DIY solar projects, each small piece moves you closer to the dream. The path to an off-grid lifestyle is personal and unique to everyone- an inherent and natural right toward greater independence.

As you implement these changes, know that every effort contributes to a larger purpose. This way of life promotes greater freedom, personal growth, and environmental stewardship. Your actions can also inspire others who seek to live more sustainably.

In closing, I would like to leave you with this one message: believe in your ability to create a life that aligns with *your* values and dreams. Off-grid living is more than a lifestyle; it is proof of your resilience and creativity. Allow the challenges and opportunities that come your way, accepting that each one brings you closer to a life of greater autonomy and fulfillment. Know that you are shaping a future that honors both your personal aspirations and the well-being of our planet. Thank you for reading, and please feel free to contact me with questions anytime!

Resources

ATO- vertical axis wind turbines www.ato.com

Battle Born Batteries- batteries, water tanks www.battlebornbatteries.com

Berkey Filters- water filtration www.berkeywaterfilter.com

BougeRV- bifacial solar panels www.bougerv.com

American Society of Dowsers www.learntodowse.com

Eco Direct- inverters www.ecodirect.com

Flojak- hand well pumps www.flojak.com

GoGreenSolar-solar panels www.gogreensolar.com

Inverter Store-inverters www.theinverterstore.com

Jackery – solar inverters www.jackery.com

Lifestraw- water filtration www.lifestraw.com

Lithium Battery Store-lithium batteries, batteries, chargers www.lithiumbatterystore.com

Micro Hydropower-engines, meters, transformers www.microhydropower.com

Tank Depot-water tanks www.tank-depot.com

Tesla- solar panels, powerwall www.tesla.com

Zero Water- water filtration www.zerowater.com

Bibliography

- *10 Essential Tips for Successful Off-Grid Living* https://www.linkedin.com/pulse/10-essential-tips-successful-off-grid-living-beginners-guide

- *11 Methods For Off-Grid Water Filtration And Purification Guide* https://homesteading.rusticskills.com/water-filters/off-grid-water-filtration-purification/

- *15 Building Products Designed to Withstand Natural ...* https://www.foxblocks.com/blog/15-building-products-designed-to-withstand-natural-disasters

- *5 Mental Health Rewards Of Embracing Minimalism ...* https://www.forbes.com/sites/traversmark/2023/06/28/5-mental-health-rewards-of-embracing-minimalism-according-to-a-psychologist/

- *6 Surprising Health Benefits of Intentional Community Living.* https://communityfinders.com/health-benefits-of-intentional-community-living/

- *6 Tips To Stay Safe During Natural Disasters - Grab-*

NewStyle. https://www.grabnewstyle.com/tips-to-stay-safe-during-natural-disasters

- *7 Tips to Restart Life in a New City | My Beautiful Adventures.* https://mybeautifuladventures.com/2024/01/16/7-tips-to-restart-life-in-a-new-city/

- *75 Bug Out Bag List Essentials [2024 Update].* https://bugoutbagacademy.com/free-bug-out-bag-list/

- *9 Plants That Naturally Repel Ticks From Your Yard.* https://www.marthastewart.com/plants-that-repel-ticks-8683172

- *A Complete Guide to Rainwater Harvesting.* https://rainwatermanagement.com/blogs/news/rainwater-harvesting?srsltid=AfmBOorg_tb5NRvEXXjtHebyY3RE8FqWBKVm0CHm1hsOw4CJxk6NbtmC

- *A Guide on Choosing The Right Sized Residential Solar System | Solar Power Direct.* https://solarpowerdirect.com.au/news/a-guide-on-choosing-the-right-sized-residential-solar-system

- *A Way to Garden with Margaret Roach – Oct 8, 2018 – Eliot Coleman on Organic Growing – ROBIN HOOD RADIO ON DEMAND AUDIO PAGE.* https://robinhoodradioondemand.com/podcast/5821/

- *Ahmadi, M., Ahmadi, M., Amiry, S., & Yona, A. (2023). Maximizing Annual Energy Yield in a Grid-Connected PV Solar Power Plant: Analysis of Seasonal Tilt Angle and Solar Tracking Strategies. Sustainability, 15(14), 11053.*

- *Attract Beneficial Garden Insects and Natural*

... https://www.motherearthnews.com/organic-gardening/pest
-control/natural-garden-predators-zm0z22jjzols/

- *Best Practices for Nutrient Management in Agronomy - Agronomy
  Magazine.* https://agronomymagazine.com/insight/best-practi
  ces-for-nutrient-management-in-agronomy/

- *Blog Post: From Analog to Digital – How Smart Off-Grid ...*
  https://www.clearbluetechnologies.com/news/blog-post-from-a
  nalog-to-digital-how-smart-off-grid-uses-advanced-technology-t
  o-make-solar-power-easier-and-more-reliable

- *Bokashi Composting:* https://www.thespruce.com/basics-of-bok
  ashi-composting-2539742

- *Bug Out Bag.* https://emergencymasters.com/emergency-gear/h
  ave-you-met-bob/

- *Building a Sustainable Prepper Garden: A Guide to Year-Round
  Harvests.* https://www.prepperpointman.com/building-a-susta
  inable-prepper-garden-a-guide-to-year-round-harvests/

- *Climate change impacts on planned supply–demand ...* https://w
  ww.nature.com/articles/s41560-023-01304-w

- *Climate Change, Health and Mosquito-Borne Diseases* https://w
  ww.ncbi.nlm.nih.gov/pmc/articles/PMC6950258/

- *Colarossi, D. (2023). Phase Change Materials as thermal energy
  storage and management in solar energy-based systems.* https://c
  ore.ac.uk/download/587759013.pdf

- *Cover design image credit to Alberto Masnovo iStock Solar panels
  and small wind turbine on the top of a roof of a house* [Stock

photo].   iStock.
https://www.istockphoto.com/photo/solar-panels-and-small-wi
nd-turbine-on-the-top-of-a-roof-of-a-house-gm1440726837-48
0626024

- *Cover design image credit to Hsvrs iStock. Vegetable garden with lettuce salad* [Stock photo]. iStock. https://www.istockphoto.com/photo/vegetable-garden-with-lettuce-salat-gm185003234-18810184

- *Cover design image credit to Josfor iStock Fresh water* [Stock photo]. iStock. https://www.istockphoto.com/photo/fresh-water-gm689636900-126973777

- *Cover design image credit to Monticello iStock Jars with variety of pickled vegetables* [Stock photo]. iStock. https://www.istockphoto.com/photo/jars-with-variety-of-pickled-vegetables-gm586373394-100667073

- *Cover design image credit to Mvltcelik iStock First aid kit and trekking equipment* [Stock photo]. iStock. https://www.istockphoto.com/photo/first-aid-kit-and-trekking-equipment-gm1381422405-442990944

- *Cover design image credit to Nadanka iStock Contributor. (n.d.). Young brown Rhode Island Red hen walking on green grass*[Stock photo].   iStock.
https://www.istockphoto.com/photo/young-brown-rhode-island-red-hen-walking-on-green-grass-gm605786624-103884613

- *Design and operation of hybrid renewable energy systems* https://www.sciencedirect.com/science/article/pii/S2211339821000010

- *World Packers discovering off-grid communities.* https://www.w orldpackers.com/articles/off-the-grid-communities

- *Ibid.*

- *DIY Solar Panel Installation: Step-by-Step Guide.* https://www. gogreensolar.com/pages/diy-solar-installation-guide

- *Do 'Natural' Insect Repellents Work?* https://www.consumerreports.org/health/insect-repelle nt/do-natural-insect-repellents-work-a6538610025/

- *drillyourownwell.com* https://drillyourownwell.com/

- *Eckhart Tolle Quote: "It is not uncommon for people to spend their whole life waiting to start living.".* https://quotefancy.com/quote/29133/Eckhart-Tolle-It-is-not-u ncommon-for-people-to-spend-their-whole-life-waiting-to-star

- *Building your own personal food forest.* https://learn.eartheasy.co m/articles/edible-perennials-building-your-personal-food-forest/

- *Emergency Preparedness Is Vital To Off-Grid Living.* https://w ww.hobbyfarms.com/emergency-preparedness-off-grid/

- *Energy Hydro Power Plants - Borderless Consulting.* https://bod lsc.com/energy-hydro-power-plants/

- *Ibid.*

- *Ibid.*

- *Ibid.*

- *Ibid.*

- *Ibid.*

- *Five Science-Backed Strategies to Build Resilience.* https://greatergood.berkeley.edu/article/item/five_scie nce_backed_strategies_to_build_resilience

- *Garden Harmony: Balancing Nature's Elements Through Proper Maintenance And Resources - Forbes Radar.* http://forbesradar.com/garden-harmony-balancing-nat ures-elements-through-proper-maintenance-and-resources/

- *Ibid*

- *Greywater Codes and Policy.* https://greywateraction.org/greyw ater-codes-and-policy/

- *Harnessing the Sun: The art of solar passive design.* https://www.inwardoutstudio.com/post/harnessing-the-s un-the-art-of-solar-passive-design

- *Homeowner's Guide to the Federal Tax Credit for Solar ...* https://www.energy.gov/eere/solar/homeowners-guide-feder al-tax-credit-solar-photovoltaics

- *Homestead Water Management: Rainwater Harvesting and ...* https://honeycreekhomestead.com/f/homestead-water-man agement-rainwater-harvesting-and-wells

- *How Do We Tackle The Energy Crunch? - Solar Power Wise.* https://solarpowerwise.com/tackle-the-energy-crunch/

- *How Does Herbal Medicine for Holistic Wellness Work?* https://acupuncturebradenton.com/how-does-herbal -medicine-for-holistic-wellness-work/

- *How Energy Use and Seasonal Changes Affect Your Solar* ... https ://www.sunnova.com/watts-up/home-solar-seasonality

- *How To Harvest rainwater.* https://homedecorish.com/2023/0 7/29/how-to-harvest-rainwater/

- *How to Prevent Mosquito and Tick Bites.* https://www.cdc.gov/ vector-borne-diseases/prevention/index.html

- *Ibid.*

- https://farm-energy.extension.org/wind-energy-for-homeowner s-farmers-and-small-businesses/#:~:text=Renewable%20Energy %20Lab.-,How%20much%20will%20it%20cost?,probably%20d oesn't%20make%20sense.

- https://pmc.ncbi.nlm.nih.gov/articles/PMC8953618/#:~:text= Nature%20walk%20have%20been%20proposed,to%20benefit% 20from%20nature%20walk.

- https://www.bayarealyme.org/about-lyme/lyme-disease-facts-sta tistics/#:~:text=Based%20on%20this%20average%20annual%20r ate%20of,627%2C927%20actual%20Lyme%20disease%20cases% 20in%202024.

- https://www.cdc.gov/ticks/tickbornediseases/TickborneDisease s-P.pdf

- https://www.irena.org/News/pressreleases/2024/Sep/Record-G rowth-Drives-Cost-Advantage-of-Renewable-Power

- https://www.pomodorotechnique.com/

- *iStock Contributor. (n.d.). Greenhouse* [Stock photo]. iStock. https://www.istockphoto.com/photo/greenhouse-gm146 4538029-4972078

- *iStock Contributor. (n.d.). Rainbarrel* [Stock Photo]. iStock. https://www.istockphoto.com/photo/blue-rain-barrel-wi th-downspout-and-stone-building-gm1281010625-379159378

- *iStock Contributor. (n.d.). Survival Hack Water Filter* [Stock Photo]. iStock. https://www.istockphoto.com/vector/survival-hack-wate r-filter-vector-ill%C3%BCstration-gm1755624657-544329930

- *iStock Contributor. (n.d.). Plantago major* [Stock photo]. iStock. https://www.istockphoto.com/photo/plantago-major-gm 928466628-254665995

- *iStock Contributor. (n.d.).Purple sun hat (Echinacea purpurea) field* [Stock photo]. iStock. https://www.istockphoto.com/photo/purple-sun-hat-ech inacea-purpurea-field-gm1166194686-321166698

- *iStock Contributor. (n.d.). Adult tick* [Stock photo]. iStock. https://www.istockphoto.com/photo/adult-tick-gm4779 93007-26872249

- *iStock Contributor. (n.d.).Water at the bottom of a newly dug well* [Stock photo]. iStock. https://www.istockphoto.com/photo/water-at-the-botto m-of-a-newly-dug-well-gm2089515826-565749910

- *iStock Contributor. (n.d.). Artesian water well in cross-section: Water resource, artesian water, and groundwater* [Stock vector]. i S t o c k .

https://www.istockphoto.com/vector/artesian-water-well-in-cro
ss-section-water-resource-artesian-water-and-groundwater-gm12
83352152-380800128

- *iStock Contributor. (n.d.). Water supply wells in residential premises: Infographics of soil layers and groundwater* [Stock vector].   iStock.
  https://www.istockphoto.com/vector/water-supply-wells-in-resi
  dential-premises-infographics-of-soil-layers-and-gm2150613468
  -571771768

- *iStock   Contributor.   (n.d.).   3D   rendering: Several   types   of   solar   panels* [Stock   photo].   iStock. https://www.istockphoto.com/photo/3d-rendering-sever
  al-type-of-solar-panel-gm1303704001-395081885

- *iStock Contributor. (n.d.). Solar panels and small wind turbine on the top of a roof of a house* [Stock photo]. iStock.
  https://www.istockphoto.com/photo/solar-panels-and-small-wi
  nd-turbine-on-the-top-of-a-roof-of-a-house-gm1440726837-48
  062602

- *Interventions to reduce loneliness and social isolation in* ... https://www.sciencedirect.com/science/article/abs/pii/S074
  3016722000237

- *Introducing   Sustainable   Companion   Planting   Techniques.* https://bytesizedblogs.com/gardening/and/landscaping
  /2023/06/21/23008.htm

- *Living   off   Grid   -   What   is   Homesteading?*
  https://www.kuhl.com/borninthemountains/living-off-grid-wh
  at-is-homesteading#:~:text=the%20other%20animals.-,Carpentr

y,and%20even%20your%20own%20house.

- *Lyme Disease.* https://igaku.co/blog/2024/07/28/lyme-disease/

- *Micro-Hydro Power: A Beginners Guide to Design and ...* https://attra.ncat.org/publication/micro-hydro-power-a-begi nners-guide-to-design-and-installation/

- *Natural Remedies: Harnessing the Power of Nature for Common Ailments.* https://ruyzfrontier.com/natural-remedies-harnessin g-the-power-of-nature-for-common-ailments/

- *Net metering.* https://ised-isde.canada.ca/site/measurement-can ada/en/mandate/net-metering

- *Off-Grid Living in Australia: How Portable Generators Enhance Sustainability.* https://spiritualfeel.com/off-grid-living-in-austr alia-how-portable-generators-enhance-sustainability/

- *Off-Grid Living: 7 Renewable Power Systems & Energy Sources.* https://greenbuildingcanada.ca/off-grid-living/

- *Outdoor Pest Control: Keeping Your Garden and Surroundings Pest-Free.* https://www.urbanpestcontrolindia.com/post/outdo or-pest-control-keeping-your-garden-and-surroundings-pest-free

- *Outdoor Programming: Insects and Animal Safeguarding - The Redwoods Group.* https://redwoodsgroup.com/resources/outdo or-programming-insects-and-animal-safeguarding-2/

- *Plant Rx: Attack of the Aphids.* https://www.thecultivationbyka t.com/post/plant-rx-attack-of-the-aphids

- *Predicting Transmission Suitability of Mosquito-Borne ...* https:/

/www.ncbi.nlm.nih.gov/pmc/articles/PMC9603533/

- *Prepping   for   the   Alien   Invasion.* https://survivalskillzone.com/prepping-for-the-alien-invasion-assess-stock-up-secure-connect-learn/

- *Preserving food without refrigeration: 3 Ways to Master.* https://natureofthenorth.co/basics/preserving-food-without-refrigeration/

- *Quotes by Ian Davis-Quotes.* https://www.azquotes.com/author/31868-Ian_Davis

- *Rainwater Harvesting: 5 Uses Nature's Water for Your Home - Plumfast.* https://plumfast.com.au/rainwater-harvesting-using-natures-water/

- *Renewable   Power   Generation   Costs   in 2022.* https://www.irena.org/Publications/2023/Aug/Renewable-Power-Generation-Costs-in-2022

- *Root Cellars: Types and Storage Tips.* https://www.almanac.com/content/root-cellars-types-and-storage-tips

- *DIY Solar Oven.* https://www.ecowatch.com/solar-oven-cooker-diy.html

- *Small Wind Guidebook - WINDExchange.* https://windexchange.energy.gov/small-wind-guidebook

- *Solar batteries - ABM (East Africa).* https://abmeastafrica.com/our-product-range/solar-batteries/

- *Solar Credit Massachusetts Archives - The Solar Guy.* http://thes

olarguyne.com/tag/solar-credit-massachusetts/

- *Solar Financing Options.* https://enphase.com/blog/homeowners/home-solar-financing-options?srsltid=AfmBOoopxucVgv2HP8OaDkbDGmp7FGoM_ZgYjHcyphUkc8Cfyi7y1KQt

- *Solar Panels.* https://physicscalculations.com/solar-panels/

- *Step-by-Step Guide to Soil Testing with Full Video.* https://www.thehomesteadeducation.com/soil-test-guide/

- *The Allure and Challenges of Off-Grid Architecture and Living.* https://architizer.com/blog/inspiration/stories/independent-design-architecture-off-grid-living/

- *The Benefits of Off Grid Living for Mental Health & Wellbeing.* https://liveoffgrid.co.uk/the-benefits-of-off-grid-living-for-mental-health-wellbeing/

- *Ibid.*

- *The Best/Worst States for You to Live Off the Grid in 2024.* https://zendure.com/blogs/news/the-10-best-states-to-live-off-the-grid

- *The Big Dig: How to Choose the Right Ground Drilling Equipment for Your Project - High Growth Scotland.* https://highgrowth.scot/the-big-dig-how-to-choose-the-right-ground-drilling-equipment-for-your-project/

- *The critical role of cyber security in off-grid technologies.* https://www.ifsecglobal.com/integrated-security/securing-the-digital-frontier-the-critical-role-of-cyber-security-in-off-grid-technologies/#:~:text=Prioritising%20cybersecurity%20in%20off%2D grid%20technologies

- *The Future of Off Grid Homes.* https://www.planradar.com/au /the-future-of-off-grid-homes/

- *The Future of Solar Energy: Trends and Innovations | Solar Pro.* https://www.solarprony.com/the-future-of-solar-energy-tr ends-and-innovations/

- *The Healing Power of Herbaceous Plants: Medicinal Herb Garden Guide - Plant Instructions.* https://somuchviral.com/herbs/the-healing-power-of-her baceous-plants-medicinal-herb-garden-guide/

- *The Legal Constraints of Off-Grid Building.* https://www.build erfinance.com/blog/legal-constraints-off-grid-building

- *The ultimate guide to starting a frugal off-grid living ... https://frugaloffgrid.com/blogs/frugal-off-grid-blog/ultimate-guid e-to-starting-a-frugal-off-grid-homestead-for-beginners?srsltid=Af mBOorgEXGd179i8do9805AJ9TNwXTw1iPWeJoH8S_xJTILk kobLAxy*

- *The Ultimate List Of 63 Must Have Off Grid Tools For The ...* https://theoffgridcabin.com/the-ultimate-list-must-have -off-grid-tools/

- *Tick Bites: Causes, Symptoms, Treatment & Prevention.* https:// my.clevelandclinic.org/health/diseases/7234-tick-bites

- *Tick Prevention and Property Management* https://www.maine.gov/dhhs/mecdc/infectious-disease/epi/vect or-borne/lyme/tick-prevention-and-property-management.sht ml

- *Tick Season: Recognizing the Signs of Lyme Disease and Taking Preventative Measures - Horizon Family Medical Group - New York.* https://www.horizonfamilymedicalgroupnewyork.com/2 023/07/13/tick-season/

- *Ticks In Dogs: Prevalence, Risks Factors, And Distribution - The Dogs Journal.* https://thedogsjournal.com/ticks-in-dogs-prevale nce-risks-factors-distribution/

- *Top 8 Off-Grid Energy Storage Companies.* https://www.verifiedmarketresearch.com/blog/top-off-grid-ener gy-storage-companies/#:~:text=Battery%20storage%20systems% 2C%20including%20lithium,in%20remote%20or%20underserve d%20areas.

- *Torn paper cover design by Freepik*

- *Trash to Treasure: Creative Ways to Repurpose Your Unwanted Items - Mesa Junk Removal.* https://removejunkmesa.com/tras h-to-treasure-creative-ways-to-repurpose-your-unwanted-items/

- *Vector-Borne Diseases.* https://www.cdc.gov/vector-borne-disea ses/index.html

- *What are the Best Battery Types for Off Grid Living?* https://bl og.ecoflow.com/us/battery-types-for-off-grid-living/

- *What are the best preventive measures against tick bites for children playing outdoors?* https://redinational.com/what-are-the-best-pr eventive-measures-against-ticks-for-children-playing-outdoors/

- *What Is a Vertical Gardening? - GardenProfy.* https://gardenpr

ofy.com/what-is-a-vertical-gardening/

- *What is the Cycle Life of a Battery? | Zitara Glossary.* https://www.zitara.com/glossary/terms/cycle-life

- *Why are some businesses today using the barter system? | Prime Trade NW.* https://primetradenw.com/why-are-some-businesses-today-using-the-barter-system/

- *Wildlife Deterrents and Repellents.* https://www.naperville.il.us/services/naperville-police-department/programs-and-services/animal-control/wildlife-issues/wildlife-deterrents-and-repellents/

www.ingramcontent.com/pod-product-compliance
Lightning Source LLC
Chambersburg PA
CBHW061806120626
46550CB00005B/2158